Rule a Wife and Have a Wife by John Fletcher

John Fletcher was born in December, 1579 in Rye, Sussex. He was baptised on December 20th.

As can be imagined details of much of his life and career have not survived and, accordingly, only a very brief indication of his life and works can be given.

Young Fletcher appears at the very young age of eleven to have entered Corpus Christi College at Cambridge University in 1591. There are no records that he ever took a degree but there is some small evidence that he was being prepared for a career in the church.

However what is clear is that this was soon abandoned as he joined the stream of people who would leave University and decamp to the more bohemian life of commercial theatre in London.

The upbringing of the now teenage Fletcher and his seven siblings now passed to his paternal uncle, the poet and minor official Giles Fletcher. Giles, who had the patronage of the Earl of Essex may have been a liability rather than an advantage to the young Fletcher. With Essex involved in the failed rebellion against Elizabeth Giles was also tainted.

By 1606 John Fletcher appears to have equipped himself with the talents to become a playwright. Initially this appears to have been for the Children of the Queen's Revels, then performing at the Blackfriars Theatre.

Fletcher's early career was marked by one significant failure; The Faithful Shepherdess, his adaptation of Giovanni Battista Guarini's Il Pastor Fido, which was performed by the Blackfriars Children in 1608.

By 1609, however, he had found his stride. With his collaborator John Beaumont, he wrote Philaster, which became a hit for the King's Men and began a profitable association between Fletcher and that company. Philaster appears also to have begun a trend for tragicomedy.

By the middle of the 1610s, Fletcher's plays had achieved a popularity that rivalled Shakespeare's and cemented the pre-eminence of the King's Men in Jacobean London. After his frequent early collaborator John Beaumont's early death in 1616, Fletcher continued working, both singly and in collaboration, until his own death in 1625. By that time, he had produced, or had been credited with, close to fifty plays.

Index of Contents

DRAMATIS PERSONAE
SCENE: Spain
PROLOGUE
ACTUS PRIMUS
SCÆNA PRIMA
ACTUS SECUNDUS
SCÆNA PRIMA
ACTUS TERTIUS
SCÆNA PRIMA

ACTUS QUARTUS
SCÆNA PRIMA
ACTUS QUINTUS
SCÆNA PRIMA
JOHN FLETCHER - A SHORT BIOGRAPHY
JOHN FLETCHER - A CONCISE BIBLIOGRAPHY

DRAMATIS PERSONAE
MEN
Duke of Medina
Don Juan De Castro, a Spanish Colonel
Aanchio   } Officers in the Army
Alonzo   }
Michael Perez, the Copper Captain
Leon, Brother to Altea, and by her contrivance married to Margarita
Cacafogo, a rich Usurer
WOMEN
Margarita, a wanton Lady, married to Leon by whom she is reclaimed
Altea, her Servant
Clara, a Spanish Ladt
Estifania, a Woman of Intrigue
An Old Woman
Maid
Visiting Ladies

SCENE: Spain

PROLOGUE

Pleasure attend ye, and about ye sit
The springs of mirth, fancy, delight and wit
To stir you up, do not your looks let fall,
Nor to remembrance our late errors call,
Because this day w' are Spaniards all again,
The story of our Play, and our Scene Spain:
The errors too, do not for this cause hate,
Now we present their wit and not their state.
Nor Ladies be not angry if you see,
A young fresh beauty, wanton and too free,
Seek to abuse her Husband, still 'tis Spain,
No such gross errors in your Kingdom raign,
W' are Vesrals all, and though we blow the fire,

We seldom make it flame up to desire,
Take no example neither to begin,
For some by precedent delight to sin:
Nor blame the Poet if he slip aside
Sometimes lasciviously if not too wide.
But hold your Fanns close, and then smile at ease,
A cruel Scene did never Lady please.
Nor Gentlemen, pray be not you displeased,
Though we present some men fool'd, some diseased,
Some drunk, some mad: we mean not you, you're free,
We taxe no farther than our Comedie,
You are our friends, sit noble then and see.

ACTUS PRIMUS

SCÆNA PRIMA

Enter **JUAN DE CASTRO**, and **MICHAEL PEREZ**.

MICHAEL PEREZ
Are your Companies full, Colonel?

JUAN DE CASTRO
No, not yet, Sir:
Nor will not be this month yet, as I reckon;
How rises your Command?

MICHAEL PEREZ
We pick up still, and as our monies hold out,
We have men come, about that time I think
We shall be full too, many young Gallants go.

JUAN DE CASTRO
And unexperienced,
The Wars are dainty dreams to young hot spirits,
Time and Experience will allay those Visions,
We have strange things to fill our numbers,
There's one Don Leon, a strange goodly fellow,
Recommended to me from some noble Friends,
For my Alferes, had you but seen his Person,
And what a Giants promise it protesteth.

MICHAEL PEREZ
I have heard of him, and that he hath serv'd before too.

JUAN DE CASTRO

But no harm done, nor never meant, Don Michael,
That came to my ears yet, ask him a question,
He blushes like a Girl, and answers little,
To the point less, he wears a Sword, a good one,
And good Cloaths too, he is whole skin'd, has no hurt yet,
Good promising hopes, I never yet heard certainly
Of any Gentleman that saw him angry.

MICHAEL PEREZ
Preserve him, he'll conclude a peace if need be,
Many as strong as he will go along with us,
That swear as valiantly as heart can wish,
Their mouths charg'd with six oaths at once, and whole ones,
That make the drunken Dutch creep into Mole-hills.

JUAN DE CASTRO
'Tis true, such we must look for: but Mich. Perez,
When heard you of Donna Margarita, the great Heiress?

MICHAEL PEREZ
I hear every hour of her, though I never saw her,
She is the main discourse: noble Don Juan de Castro,
How happy were that man could catch this Wench up,
And live at ease! she is fair, and young, and wealthy,
Infinite wealthy, and as gracious too
In all her entertainments, as men report.

JUAN DE CASTRO
But she is proud, Sir, that I know for certain,
And that comes seldome without wantonness,
He that shall marry her, must have a rare hand.

MICHAEL PEREZ
Would I were married, I would find that Wisdom,
With a light rein to rule my Wife: if ever Woman
Of the most subtile mould went beyond me,
I would give the Boys leave to whoot me out o'th' Parish.

[Enter a **SERVANT**.

SERVANT
Sir, there be two Gentlewomen attend to speak
With you.

JUAN DE CASTRO
Wait on 'em in.

MICHAEL PEREZ

Are they two handsome Women?

SERVANT
They seem so, very handsom, but they are vail'd, Sir.

MICHAEL PEREZ
Thou put'st sugar in my mouth, how it melts with me!
I love a sweet young Wench.

JUAN DE CASTRO
Wait on them in I say.

[Exit **SERVANT**.

MICHAEL PEREZ
Don Juan.

JUAN DE CASTRO
How you itch, Michael! how you burnish!
Will not this Souldiers heat out of your bones yet,
Do your Eyes glow now?

MICHAEL PEREZ
There be two.

JUAN DE CASTRO
Say honest, what shame have you then?

MICHAEL PEREZ
I would fain see that,
I have been in the Indies twice, and have seen strange things,
But two honest Women;—one I read of once.

JUAN DE CASTRO
Prithee be modest.

MICHAEL PEREZ
I'll be any thing.

[Enter **SERVANT**, **DONNA CLARA**, and **ESTIFANIA**, vail'd.

JUAN DE CASTRO
You are welcome Ladies.

MICHAEL PEREZ
Both hooded, I like 'em well though,
They come not for advice in Law sure hither;
May be they would learn to raise the Pike,

I am for 'em: they are very modest, 'tis a fine Preludium.

JUAN DE CASTRO
With me, or with this Gentleman,
Would you speak, Lady?

CLARA
With you, Sir, as I guess, Juan de Castro.

MICHAEL PEREZ
Her Curtain opens, she is a pretty Gentlewoman.

JUAN DE CASTRO
I am the Man, and shall be bound to Fortune,
I may do any service to your Beauties.

CLARA
Captain, I hear you are marching down to Flanders,
To serve the Catholick King.

JUAN DE CASTRO
I am sweet Lady.

CLARA
I have a Kinsman, and a noble Friend,
Imploy'd in those Wars, may be, Sir, you know him,
Don Campusano Captain of Carbines,
To whom I would request your Nobleness,
To give this poor Remembrance.

[Gives a Letter.

JUAN DE CASTRO
I shall do it,
I know the Gentleman, a most worthy Captain.

CLARA
Something in private.

JUAN DE CASTRO
Step aside: I'll serve thee.

[Exit **JUAN DE CASTRO** and **CLARA**.

MICHAEL PEREZ
Prithee let me see thy face.

ESTIFANIA

Sir, you must pardon me,
Women of our sort, that maintain fair memories,
And keep suspect off from their Chastities,
Had need wear thicker Vails.

MICHAEL PEREZ
I am no blaster of a Ladies Beauty,
Nor bold intruder on her special favours,
I know how tender Reputation is,
And with what guards it ought to be preserv'd, Lady,
You may to me.

ESTIFANIA
You must excuse me, Seignior, I come
Not here to sell my self.

MICHAEL PEREZ
As I am a Gentleman, by the honour of a Souldier.

ESTIFANIA
I believe you,
I pray you be civil, I believe you would see me,
And when you have seen me I believe you will like me,
But in a strange place, to a stranger too,
As if I came on purpose to betray you,
Indeed I will not.

MICHAEL PEREZ
I shall love you dearly,
And 'tis a sin to fling away affection,
I have no Mistress, no desire to honour
Any but you, will not this Oyster open?
I know not, you have struck me with your modesty;
She will draw sure; so deep, and taken from me
All the desire I might bestow on others,
Quickly before they come.

ESTIFANIA
Indeed I dare not:
But since I see you are so desirous, Sir,
To view a poor face that can merit nothing
But your Repentance.

MICHAEL PEREZ
It must needs be excellent.

ESTIFANIA
And with what honesty you ask it of me,

When I am gone let your man follow me,
And view what house I enter, thither come,
For there I dare be bold to appear open:
And as I like your vertuous carriage then,

[Enter **JUAN DE CASTRO, DONNA CLARA**, a **SERVANT**.

I shall be able to give welcome to you;
She hath done her business, I must take my leave, Sir.

MICHAEL PEREZ
I'll kiss your fair white hand and thank you, Lady.
My man shall wait, and I shall be your Servant;
Sirrah, come near, hark.

SERVANT
I shall do it faithfully.

[Exit.

JUAN DE CASTRO
You will command me no more services?

CLARA
To be careful of your noble health, dear Sir,
That I may ever honour you.

JUAN DE CASTRO
I thank you,
And kiss your hands, wait on the Ladies down there.

[Exeunt **LADIES** and **SERVANTS**.

MICHAEL PEREZ
You had the honour to see the face that came to you?

JUAN DE CASTRO
And 'twas a fair one; what was yours, Don Michael?

MICHAEL PEREZ
Mine was i'th' clipse, and had a Cloud drawn over it.
But I believe well, and I hope 'tis handsome,
She had a hand would stir a holy Hermite.

JUAN DE CASTRO
You know none of 'em?

MICHAEL PEREZ

No.

JUAN DE CASTRO
Then I do, Captain,
But I'll say nothing till I see the proof on't,
Sit close Don Perez, or your Worship's caught.
I fear a Flye.

MICHAEL PEREZ
Were those she brought Love-Letters?

JUAN DE CASTRO
A Packet to a Kinsman now in Flanders,
Yours was very modest methought.

MICHAEL PEREZ
Some young unmanag'd thing,
But I may live to see—

JUAN DE CASTRO
'Tis worth experience,
Let's walk abroad and view our Companies.

[Exeunt.

[Enter **SANCHIO** and **ALONZO**.

SANCHIO
What, are you for the Wars, Alonzo?

ALONZO
It may be I,
It may be no, e'n as the humour takes me.
If I find peace amongst the female Creatures,
And easie entertainment, I'll stay at home,
I am not so far obliged yet to long Marches
And mouldy Biskets, to run mad for Honour,
When you are all gone I have my choice before me.

SANCHIO
Of which Hospital thou wilt sweat in; wilt thou
Never leave whoring?

ALONZO
There is less danger in't than gunning, Sanchio,
Though we be shot sometimes, the shot's not mortal,
Besides, it breaks no limbs.

SANCHIO
But it disables 'em,
Dost thou see how thou pull'st thy legs after thee, as they
Hung by points.

ALONZO
Better to pull 'em thus than walk on wooden ones,
Serve bravely for a Billet to support me.

SANCHIO
Fye, fye, 'tis base.

ALONZO
Dost thou count it base to suffer?
Suffer abundantly? 'tis the Crown of Honour;
You think it nothing to lie twenty days
Under a Surgeons hands that has no mercy.

SANCHIO
As thou hast done I am sure, but I perceive now
Why you desire to stay, the orient Heiress,
The Margarita, Sir,

ALONZO
I would I had her.

SANCHIO
They say she will marry.

ALONZO
I think she will.

SANCHIO
And marry suddenly, as report goes too,
She fears her Youth will not hold out, Alonzo.

ALONZO
I would I had the sheathing on't.

SANCHIO
They say too
She has a greedy eye that must be fed
With more than one mans meat.

ALONZO
Would she were mine,
I would cater for her well enough; but Sanchio,
There be too many great men that adore her,

Princes, and Princes fellows, that claim priviledge.

SANCHIO
Yet those stand off i'th' way of marriage,
To be tyed to a man's pleasure is a second labour.

ALONZO
She has bought a brave house here in town.

SANCHIO
I have heard so.

ALONZO
If she convert it now to pious uses,
And bid poor Gentlemen welcome.

SANCHIO
When comes she to it?

ALONZO
Within these two days, she is in the Country yet,
And keeps the noblest House.

SANCHIO
Then there's some hope of her,
Wilt thou go my way?

ALONZO
No, no, I must leave you,
And repair to an old Gentlewoman
That has credit with her, that can speak a good word.

SANCHIO
Send thee good fortune, but make thy Body sound first.

ALONZO
I am a Souldier,
And too sound a Body becomes me not;
Farewel, Sanchio.

[Exeunt.

[Enter a **SERVANT** of Michael Perez.

SERVANT
'Tis this or that house, or I have lost my aim,
They are both fair buildings, she walked plaguy fast,

[Enter **ESTIFANIA**.

And hereabouts I lost her; stay, that's she,
'Tis very she,—she makes me a low court'sie,
Let me note the place, the street I well remember.

[Exit.

She is in again, certain some noble Lady.
How happy should I be if she love my master:
A wondrous goodly house, here are brave lodgings,
And I shall sleep now like an Emperour,
And eat abundantly: I thank my fortune,
I'll back with speed, and bring him happy tidings.

[Exit.

[Enter three old **LADIES**.

FIRST LADY
What should it mean, that in such haste
We are sent for?

SECOND LADY
Belike the Lady Margaret has some business
She would break to us in private.

THIRD LADY
It should seem so.
'Tis a good Lady, and a wise young Lady.

SECOND LADY
And vertuous enough too I warrant ye
For a young Woman of her years; 'tis pity
To load her tender Age with too much Vertue.

THIRD LADY
'Tis more sometimes than we can well away with.

[Enter **ALTEA**.

ALTEA
Good morrow, Ladies.

ALL
'Morrow, my good Madam.

FIRST LADY

How does the sweet young Beauty, Lady Margaret?

SECOND LADY
Has she slept well after her walk last night?

FIRST LADY
Are her dreams gentle to her mind?

ALTEA
All's well,
She's very well, she sent for you thus suddenly
To give her counsel in a business
That much concerns her.

SECOND LADY
She does well and wisely,
To ask the counsel of the ancientst, Madam,
Our years have run through many things she knows not.

ALTEA
She would fain marry.

FIRST LADY
'Tis a proper calling,
And well beseems her years, who would she yoke with?

ALTEA
That's left to argue on, I pray come in
And break your fast, drink a good cup or two,
To strengthen your understandings, then she'l tell ye.

SECOND LADY
And good wine breeds good counsel.
We'l yield to ye.

[Exeunt.

[Enter **JUAN DE CASTRO** and **LEON**.

JUAN DE CASTRO
Have you seen any service?

LEON
Yes.

JUAN DE CASTRO
Where?

LEON
Every where.

JUAN DE CASTRO
What office bore ye?

LEON
None, I was not worthy.

JUAN DE CASTRO
What Captains know you?

LEON
None, they were above me.

JUAN DE CASTRO
Were you never hurt?

LEON
Not that I well remember,
But once I stole a Hen, and then they beat me;
Pray ask me no long questions, I have an ill memory.

JUAN DE CASTRO
This is an Asse, did you never draw your sword yet?

LEON
Not to do any harm I thank Heaven for't.

JUAN DE CASTRO
Nor ne'r ta'ne prisoner?

LEON
No, I ran away,
For I had ne'r no mony to redeem me.

JUAN DE CASTRO
Can you endure a Drum?

LEON
It makes my head ake.

JUAN DE CASTRO
Are you not valiant when you are drunk?

LEON
I think not, but I am loving Sir.

JUAN DE CASTRO
What a lump is this man,
Was your Father wise?

LEON
Too wise for me I'm sure,
For he gave all he had to my younger Brother.

JUAN DE CASTRO
That was no foolish part I'le bear you witness.
Canst thou lye with a woman?

LEON
I think I could make shift Sir,
But I am bashfull.

JUAN DE CASTRO
In the night?

LEON
I know not,
Darkness indeed may do some good upon me.

JUAN DE CASTRO
Why art thou sent to me to be my officer,
I, and commended too, when thou darst not fight?

LEON
There be more officers of my opinion,
Or I am cozen'd Sir, men that talk more too.

JUAN DE CASTRO
How wilt thou scape a bullet?

LEON
Why by chance,
They aim at honourable men, alas I am none Sir.

JUAN DE CASTRO
This fellow has some doubts in's talk that strike me,

[Enter **ALONZO**.

He cannot be all fool: welcom Alonzo.

ALONZO
What have you got there, temperance into your company?
The spirit of peace? we shall have wars

[Enter **CACAFOGO**.

By th'ounce then. O here's another pumpion,
Let him loose for luck sake, the cram'd son
Of a stay'd Usurer, Cacafogo, both their brains butter'd,
Cannot make two spoonfulls.

CACAFOGO
My Father's dead: I am a man of war too,
Monyes, demesns; I have ships at sea too,
Captains.

JUAN DE CASTRO
Take heed o'th' Hollanders, your ships may leak else.

CACAFOGO
I scorn the Hollanders, they are my drunkards.

ALONZO
Put up your gold Sir, I'le borrow it else.

CACAFOGO
I am satisfied, you shall not,
Come out, I know thee, meet mine anger instantly.

LEON
I never wrong'd ye.

CACAFOGO
Thou hast wrong'd mine honor,
Thou look'dst upon my Mistris thrice lasciviously,
I'le make it good.

JUAN DE CASTRO
Do not heat your self, you will surfeit.

CACAFOGO
Thou wan'st my mony too, with a pair of base bones,
In whom there was no truth, for which I beat thee,
I beat thee much, now I will hurt thee dangerously.
This shall provoke thee.

[He strikes.

ALONZO
You struck too low by a foot Sir.

JUAN DE CASTRO
You must get a ladder when you would beat
This fellow.

LEON
I cannot chuse but kick again, pray pardon me.

CACAFOGO
Had'st thou not ask'd my pardon, I had kill'd thee,
I leave thee as a thing despis'd, assoles manus a vostra siniare
a Maistre.

[Exit **CACAFOGO**.

ALONZO
You have scap'd by miracle, there is not in all Spain,
A spirit of more fury than this fire drake.

LEON
I see he is hasty, and I would give him leave
To beat me soundly if he would take my bond.

JUAN DE CASTRO
What shall I do with this fellow?

ALONZO
Turn him off,
He will infect the camp with cowardise,
If he goe with thee.

JUAN DE CASTRO
About some week hence Sir,
If I can hit upon no abler officer,
You shall hear from me.

LEON
I desire no better.

[Exit.

[Enter **ESTIFANIA** and **PEREZ**.

MICHAEL PEREZ
You have made me now too bountifull amends, Lady
For your strict carriage when you saw me first,
These beauties were not meant to be conceal'd,
It was a wrong to hide so sweet an object,
I cou'd now chide ye, but it shall be thus,

No other anger ever touch your sweetness.

ESTIFANIA
You appear to me so honest, and so civil,
Without a blush Sir, I dare bid ye welcom.

MICHAEL PEREZ
Now let me ask your name.

ESTIFANIA
'Tis Estifanie, the heir of this poor place.

MICHAEL PEREZ
Poor do you call it?
There's nothing that I cast mine eyes upon,
But shews both rich and admirable, all the rooms
Are hung as if a Princess were to dwell here,
The Gardens, Orchards, every thing so curious:
Is all that plate your own too?

ESTIFANIA
'Tis but little,
Only for present use, I have more and richer,
When need shall call, or friends compel me use it,
The sutes you see of all the upper chamber,
Are those that commonly adorn the house,
I think I have besides, as fair, as civil,
As any town in Spain can parallel.

MICHAEL PEREZ
Now if she be not married, I have some hopes.
Are you a maid?

ESTIFANIA
You make me blush to answer,
I ever was accounted so to this hour,
And that's the reason that I live retir'd Sir.

MICHAEL PEREZ
Then would I counsel you to marry presently,
(If I can get her, I am made for ever)
For every year you lose, you lose a beauty,
A Husband now, an honest careful Husband,
Were such a comfort: will ye walk above stairs?

ESTIFANIA
This place will fit our talk, 'tis fitter far Sir,
Above there are day-beds, and such temptations

I dare not trust Sir.

MICHAEL PEREZ
She is excellent wise withal too.

ESTIFANIA
You nam'd a husband, I am not so strict Sir,
Nor ti'd unto a Virgins solitariness,
But if an honest, and a noble one,
Rich, and a souldier, for so I have vowed he shall be,
Were offer'd me, I think I should accept him,
But above all he must love.

MICHAEL PEREZ
He were base else,
There's comfort ministred in the word souldier,
How sweetly should I live!

ESTIFANIA
I am not so ignorant, but that I know well,
How to be commanded,
And how again to make my self obey'd Sir,
I waste but little, I have gather'd much,
My rial not the less worth, when 'tis spent,
If spent by my direction, to please my Husband,
I hold it as indifferent in my duty,
To be his maid i'th' kitchen, or his Cook,
As in the Hall to know my self the Mistris.

MICHAEL PEREZ
Sweet, rich, and provident, now fortune stick
To me; I am a Souldier, and a bachelour, Lady,
And such a wife as you, I cou'd love infinitely,
They that use many words, some are deceitfull,
I long to be a Husband, and a good one,
For 'tis most certain I shall make a president
For all that follow me to love their Ladies,
I am young you see, able I would have you think too,
If't please you know, try me before you take me.
'Tis true I shall not meet in equal wealth
With ye, but Jewels, Chains, such as the war
Has given me, a thousand Duckets I dare
Presume on in ready gold, now as your
Care may handle it, as rich cloths too, as
Any he bears arms Lady.

ESTIFANIA
You are a true gentleman, and fair, I see by ye,

And such a man I had rather take.

MICHAEL PEREZ
Pray do so, I'le have a Priest o'th' sudden.

ESTIFANIA
And as suddenly you will repent too.

MICHAEL PEREZ
I'le be hang'd or drown'd first,
By this and this, and this kiss.

ESTIFANIA
You are a Flatterer,
But I must say there was something when I saw you
First, in that most noble face, that stirr'd my fancy.

MICHAEL PEREZ
I'le stir it better e're you sleep sweet Lady,
I'le send for all my trunks and give up all to ye,
Into your own dispose, before I bed ye,
And then sweet wench.

ESTIFANIA
You have the art to cozen me.

[Exeunt.

ACTUS SECUNDUS

SCÆNA PRIMA

Enter **MARGARITA** and two **LADIES** and **ALTEA**.

MARGARITA
Sit down and give me your opinions seriously.

FIRST LADY
You say you have a mind to marry Lady.

MARGARITA
'Tis true, I have for to preserve my credit,
Yet not so much for that as for my state Ladies,
Conceive me right, there lies the main o'th' question,
Credit I can redeem, mony will imp it,
But when my monie's gone, when the law shall

Seize that, and for incontinency strip me
Of all.

FIRST LADY
Do you find your body so malitious that way?

MARGARITA
I find it as all bodies are that are young and lusty,
Lazy, and high fed, I desire my pleasure,
And pleasure I must have.

SECOND LADY
'Tis fit you should have,
Your years require it, and 'tis necessary,
As necessary as meat to a young Lady,
Sleep cannot nourish more.

FIRST LADY
But might not all this be, and keep ye single.
You take away variety in marriage,
The abundance of the pleasure you are bar'd then,
Is't not abundance that you aim at?

MARGARITA
Yes why was I made a woman?

SECOND LADY
And every day a new?

MARGARITA
Why fair and young but to use it?

FIRST LADY
You are still i'th' right, why would you marry then?

ALTEA
Because a husband stops all doubts in this point,
And clears all passages.

SECOND LADY
What Husband mean ye?

ALTEA
A Husband of an easy faith, a fool,
Made by her wealth, and moulded to her pleasure,
One though he see himself become a monster,
Shall hold the door, and entertain the maker.

SECOND LADY
You grant there may be such a man.

FIRST LADY
Yes marry, but how to bring 'em to this rare Perfection.

SECOND LADY
They must be chosen so, things of no honour,
Nor outward honesty.

MARGARITA
No 'tis no matter,
I care not what they are, so they be lusty.

SECOND LADY
Me thinks now a rich Lawyer, some such fellow,
That carries credit, and a face of awe,
But lies with nothing but his clients business.

MARGARITA
No there's no trusting them, they are too subtil,
The Law has moulded 'em of natural mischief.

FIRST LADY
Then some grave governor,
Some man of honour, yet an easy man.

MARGARITA
If he have honour I am undone, I'le none such,
I'le have a lusty man, honour will cloy me..br

ALTEA
'Tis fit ye should Lady;
And to that end, with search and wit and labour,
I have found one out, a right one and a perfect,
He is made as strong as brass, is of brave years too,
And doughty of complexion.

MARGARITA
Is he a Gentleman?

ALTEA
Yes and a souldier, as gentle as you would wish him,
A good fellow, wears good cloaths.

MARGARITA
Those I'le allow him,
They are for my credit, does he understand

But little?

ALTEA
Very little.

MARGARITA
'Tis the better,
Have not the wars bred him up to anger?

ALONZO
No, he will not quarrel with a dog that bites him,
Let him be drunk or sober, is one silence.

MARGARITA
H'as no capacity what honor is?
For that's the Souldiers god.

ALTEA
Honour's a thing too subtil for his wisdom,
If honour lye in eating, he is right honourable.

MARGARITA
Is he so goodly a man do you say?

ALTEA
As you shall see Lady,
But to all this is but a trunk.

MARGARITA
I would have him so,
I shall adde branches to him to adorn him,
Goe, find me out this man, and let me see him,
If he be that motion that you tell me of,
And make no more noise, I shall entertain him,
Let him be here.

ALTEA
He shall attend your Ladiship.

[Exeunt.

[Enter **JUAN DE CASTRO**, **ALONZO** and **PEREZ**.

JUAN DE CASTRO
Why thou art not married indeed?

MICHAEL PEREZ
No, no, pray think so,

Alas I am a fellow of no reckoning,
Not worth a Ladies eye.

ALONZO
Wou'dst thou steal a fortune,
And make none of all thy friends acquainted with it,
Nor bid us to thy wedding?

MICHAEL PEREZ
No indeed,
There was no wisdom in't, to bid an Artist,
An old seducer to a femal banquet,
I can cut up my pye without your instructions.

JUAN DE CASTRO
Was it the wench i'th' veil?

MICHAEL PEREZ
Basto 'twas she,
The prettiest Rogue that e're you look'd upon,
The lovingst thief.

JUAN DE CASTRO
And is she rich withal too?

MICHAEL PEREZ
A mine, a mine, there is no end of wealth Coronel,
I am an asse, a bashfull fool, prethee Coronel,
How do thy companies fill now?

JUAN DE CASTRO
You are merry Sir,
You intend a safer war at home belike now.

MICHAEL PEREZ
I do not think I shall fight much this year Coronel,
I find my self given to my ease a little,
I care not if I sell my foolish company,
They are things of hazard.

ALONZO
How it angers me,
This fellow at first fight should win a Lady,
A rich young wench, and I that have consum'd
My time and art in searching out their subtleties,
Like a fool'd Alchymist blow up my hopes still?
When shall we come to thy house and be freely merry?

MICHAEL PEREZ
When I have manag'd her a little more,
I have an house to entertain an army.

ALONZO
If thy wife be fair, thou wilt have few less
Come to thee.

MICHAEL PEREZ
But where they'l get entertainment is the point Signior.
I beat no Drum.

ALONZO
You need none but her taber,
May be I'le march after a month or two,
To get me a fresh stomach. I find Coronel
A wantonness in wealth, methinks I agree not with,
'Tis such a trouble to be married too,
And have a thousand things of great importance,
Jewels and plates, and fooleries molest me,
To have a mans brains whimsied with his wealth:
Before I walk'd contentedly.

[Enter **SERVANT**.

SERVANT
My Mistris Sir is sick, because you are absent,
She mourns and will not eat.

MICHAEL PEREZ
Alas my Jewel,
Come I'le goe with thee, Gentlemen your fair leaves,
You see I am ti'd a little to my yoke,
Pray pardon me, would ye had both such loving wives.

JUAN DE CASTRO
I thank ye

[Exit **PEREZ**, **SERVANT**.

For your old boots, never be blank Alonzo,
Because this fellow has outstript thy fortune,
Tell me ten daies hence what he is, and how
The gracious state of matrimony stands with him,
Come, let's to dinner, when Margarita comes
We'l visit both, it may be then your fortune.

[Exeunt.

[Enter **MARGARITA**, **ALTEA** and **LADIES**.

MARGARITA
Is he come?

ALTEA
Yes Madam, h'as been here this half hour,
I have question'd him of all that you can ask him,
And find him as fit as you had made the man,
He will make the goodliest shadow for iniquity.

MARGARITA
Have ye searcht him Ladies?

OMNES
Is a man at all points, a likely man.

MARGARITA
Call him in Altea.

[Exit **LADY**.

[Enter **LEON**, **ALTEA**.

A man of a good presence, pray ye come this way,
Of a lusty body, is his mind so tame?

ALTEA
Pray ye question him, and if you find him not
Fit for your purpose, shake him off, there's no harm
Done.

MARGARITA
Can you love a young Lady? How he blushes!

ALTEA
Leave twirling of your hat, and hold your head up,
And speak to'th' Lady.

LEON
Yes, I think I can,
I must be taught, I know not what it means Madam.

MARGARITA
You shall be taught, and can you when she pleases
Go ride abroad, and stay a week or two?
You shall have men and horses to attend ye,

And mony in your purse.

LEON
Yes I love riding,
And when I am from home I am so merry.

MARGARITA
Be as merry as you will: can you as handsomely
When you are sent for back, come with obedience,
And doe your dutie to the Lady loves you?

LEON
Yes sure, I shall.

MARGARITA
And when you see her friends here,
Or noble kinsmen, can you entertain
Their servants in the Celler, and be busied,
And hold your peace, what e're you see or hear of?

LEON
'Twere fit I were hang'd else.

MARGARITA
Let me try your kisses,
How the fool shakes, I will not eat ye Sir,
Beshrew my heart he kisses wondrous manly,
Can ye doe any thing else?

LEON
Indeed I know not;
But if your Ladiship will please to instruct me,
Sure I shall learn.

MARGARITA
You shall then be instructed:
If I should be this Lady that affects ye,
Nay say I marry ye?

ALTEA
Hark to the Lady.

MARGARITA
What mony have ye?

LEON
None Madam, nor friends,
I wou'd doe any thing to serve your Ladiship.

MARGARITA
You must not look to be my Mr Sir,
Nor talk i'th' house as though you wore the breeches,
No, nor command in any thing.

LEON
I will not,
Alas I am not able, I have no wit Madam.

MARGARITA
Nor do not labour to arrive at any,
'Twill spoil your head, I take ye upon charity,
And like a Servant ye must be unto me,
As I behold your duty I shall love ye,
And as you observe me, I may chance lye with ye,
Can you mark these?

LEON
Yes indeed forsooth.

MARGARITA
There is one thing,
That if I take ye in I put ye from me,
Utterly from me, you must not be sawcy,
No, nor at any time familiar with me,
Scarce know me, when I call ye not.

LEON
I will not, alas I never knew my self sufficiently.

MARGARITA
Nor must not now.

LEON
I'le be a Dog to please ye.

MARGARITA
Indeed you must fetch and carry as I appoint ye.

LEON
I were to blame else.

MARGARITA
Kiss me again; a strong fellow,
There is a vigor in his lips: if you see me
Kiss any other, twenty in an hour Sir,
You must not start, nor be offended.

LEON
No, if you kiss a thousand I shall be contented,
It will the better teach me how to please ye.

ALTEA
I told ye Madam.

MARGARITA
'Tis the man I wisht for; the less you speak.

LEON
I'le never speak again Madam,
But when you charge me, then I'le speak softly too.

MARGARITA
Get me a Priest, I'le wed him instantly,
But when you are married Sir, you must wait
Upon me, and see you observe my laws.

LEON
Else you shall hang me.

MARGARITA
I'le give ye better clothes when you deserve 'em,
Come in, and serve for witness.

OMNES
We shall Madam.

MARGARITA
And then away toth' city presently,
I'le to my new house and new company.

LEON
A thousand crowns are thine, and I am a made man.

ALTEA
Do not break out too soon.

LEON
I know my time wench.

[Exeunt.

[Enter **CLARA** and **ESTIFANIA** with a paper.

CLARA

What, have you caught him?

ESTIFANIA
Yes.

CLARA
And do you find him
A man of those hopes that you aim'd at?

ESTIFANIA
Yes too,
And the most kind man, and the ablest also
To give a wife content, he is sound as old wine,
And to his soundness rises on the pallat,
And there's the man; find him rich too Clara.

CLARA
Hast thou married him?

ESTIFANIA
What dost thou think I fish without a bait wench?
I bob for fools? he is mine own, I have him,
I told thee what would tickle him like a trout,
And as I cast it so I caught him daintily,
And all he has I have 'stowed at my devotion.

CLARA
Does thy Lady know this? she is coming now to town,
Now to live here in this house.

ESTIFANIA
Let her come,
She shall be welcom, I am prepar'd for her,
She is mad sure if she be angry at my fortune,
For what I have made bold.

CLARA
Dost thou not love him?

ESTIFANIA
Yes, intirely well,
As long as there he staies and looks no farther
Into my ends, but when he doubts, I hate him,
And that wise hate will teach me how to cozen him:
How to decline their wives, and curb their manners,
To put a stern and strong reyn to their natures,
And holds he is an Asse not worth acquaintance,
That cannot mould a Devil to obedience,

I owe him a good turn for these opinions,
And as I find his temper I may pay him,

[Enter **PEREZ**.

O here he is, now you shall see a kind man.

MICHAEL PEREZ
My Estifania, shall we to dinner lamb?
I know thou stay'st for me.

ESTIFANIA
I cannot eat else.

MICHAEL PEREZ
I never enter but me thinks a Paradise
Appears about me.

ESTIFANIA
You are welcom to it Sir.

MICHAEL PEREZ
I think I have the sweetest seat in Spain wench,
Me thinks the richest too, we'l eat i'th' garden
In one o'th' arbours, there 'tis cool and pleasant,
And have our wine cold in the running fountain.
Who's that?

ESTIFANIA
A friend of mine Sir.

MICHAEL PEREZ
Of what breeding?

ESTIFANIA
A Gentlewoman Sir.

MICHAEL PEREZ
What business has she?
Is she a learned woman i'th' Mathematicks,
Can she tell fortunes?

ESTIFANIA
More than I know Sir.

MICHAEL PEREZ
Or has she e're a letter from a kinswoman,
That must be delivered in my absence wife,

Or comes she from the Doctor to salute ye,
And learn your health? she looks not like a confessor.

ESTIFANIA
What need all this, why are you troubled Sir?
What do you suspect, she cannot cuckold ye,
She is a woman Sir, a very woman.

MICHAEL PEREZ
Your very woman may do very well Sir
Toward the matter, for though she cannot perform it
In her own person, she may do it by Proxie,
Your rarest jugglers work still by conspiracy.

ESTIFANIA
Cry ye mercy husband, you are jealous then,
And happily suspect me.

MICHAEL PEREZ
No indeed wife.

ESTIFANIA
Me thinks you should not till you have more cause
And clearer too: I am sure you have heard say husband,
A woman forced will free her self through Iron,
A happy, calm, and good wife discontented
May be taught tricks.

MICHAEL PEREZ
No, no, I do but jest with ye.

ESTIFANIA
To morrow friend I'le see you.

CLARA
I shall leave ye
Till then, and pray all may goe sweetly with ye.

[Exit.

ESTIFANIA
Why where's this girle, whose at the door?

[Knock.

MICHAEL PEREZ
Who knocks there?
Is't for the King ye come, you knock so boisterously?

[Look to the door.

[Enter **MAID**.

MAID
My Lady, as I live Mistris, my Ladie's come,
She's at the door, I peept through, and I saw her,
And a stately company of Ladies with her.

ESTIFANIA
This was a week too soon, but I must meet with her,
And set a new wheel going, and a subtile one,
Must blind this mighty Mars, or I am ruin'd.

MICHAEL PEREZ
What are they at door?

ESTIFANIA
Such my Michael
As you may bless the day they enter'd there,
Such for our good.

MICHAEL PEREZ
'Tis well.

ESTIFANIA
Nay, 'twill be better
If you will let me but dispose the business,
And be a stranger to it, and not disturb me,
What have I now to do but to advance your fortune?

MICHAEL PEREZ
Doe, I dare trust thee, I am asham'd I am angry,
I find thee a wise young wife.

ESTIFANIA
I'le wise your worship
Before I leave ye, pray ye walk by and say nothing,
Only salute them, and leave the rest to me Sir,
I was born to make ye a man.

MICHAEL PEREZ
The Rogue speaks heartily,
Her good will colours in her cheeks, I am born to love her,
I must be gentler to these tender natures,
A Souldiers rude harsh words befit not Ladies,
Nor must we talk to them as we talk to

Our Officers, I'le give her way, for 'tis for me she
Works now, I am husband, heir, and all she has.

[Enter **MARGARITA, ESTIFANIA, LEON, ALTEA** and **LADIES.**

Who are these, what flanting things, a woman
Of rare presence! excellent fair, this is too big
For a bawdy house, too open seated too.

ESTIFANIA
My Husband, Lady.

MARGARITA
You have gain'd a proper man.

MICHAEL PEREZ
What e're I am, I am your servant Lady.
kisses.

ESTIFANIA
Sir, be rul'd now,
And I shall make ye rich, this is my cousin,
That Gentleman dotes on her, even to death, see how he observes her.

MICHAEL PEREZ
She is a goodly woman.

ESTIFANIA
She is a mirrour,
But she is poor, she were for a Princes side else,
This house she has brought him too as to her own,
And presuming upon me, and upon my courtesie.
Conceive me short, he knows not but she is wealthy,
Or if he did know otherwise, 'twere all one,
He is so far gone.

MICHAEL PEREZ
Forward, she has a rare face.

ESTIFANIA
This we must carry with discretion Husband,
And yield unto her for four daies.

MICHAEL PEREZ
Yield our house up, our goods and wealth?

ESTIFANIA
All this is but in seeming,

To milk the lover on, do you see this writing,
I a year when they are married
Has she sealed to for our good; the time's unfit now,
I'le shew it you to morrow.

MICHAEL PEREZ
All the house?

ESTIFANIA
All, all, and we'l remove too, to confirm him,
They'l into th' country suddenly again
After they are matcht, and then she'l open to him.

MICHAEL PEREZ
The whole possession wife? look what you doe,
A part o'th' house.

ESTIFANIA
No, no, they shall have all,
And take their pleasure too, 'tis for our 'vantage.
Why, what's four daies? had you a Sister Sir,
A Niece or Mistris that required this courtesie,
And should I make a scruple to do you good?

MICHAEL PEREZ
If easily it would come back.

ESTIFANIA
I swear Sir,
As easily as it came on, is't not pity
To let such a Gentlewoman for a little help—
You give away no house.

MICHAEL PEREZ
Clear but that question.

ESTIFANIA
I'le put the writings into your hand.

MICHAEL PEREZ
Well then.

ESTIFANIA
And you shall keep them safe.

MICHAEL PEREZ
I am satisfied; wou'd I had the wench so too.

ESTIFANIA
When she has married him,
So infinite his love is linkt unto her,
You, I, or any one that helps at this pinch
May have Heaven knows what.

MICHAEL PEREZ
I'le remove the goods straight,
And take some poor house by, 'tis but for four days.

ESTIFANIA
I have a poor old friend; there we'l be.

MICHAEL PEREZ
'Tis well then.

ESTIFANIA
Goe handsom off, and leave the house clear.

MICHAEL PEREZ
Well.

ESTIFANIA
That little stuff we'l use shall follow after;
And a boy to guide ye, peace and we are made both.

MARGARITA
Come, let's goe in, are all the rooms kept sweet wench?

ESTIFANIA
They are sweet and neat.

[Exit **PEREZ**.

MARGARITA
Why where's your Husband?

ESTIFANIA
Gone Madam.
When you come to your own he must give place Lady.

MARGARITA
Well, send you joy, you would not let me know't,
Yet I shall not forget ye.

ESTIFANIA
Thank your Ladyship.

[Exeunt.

Enter **MARGARITA, ALTEA** and **BOY**.

ALTEA
Are you at ease now, is your heart at rest,
Now you have got a shadow, an umbrella
To keep the scorching worlds opinion
From your fair credit.

MARGARITA
I am at peace Altea,
If he continue but the same he shews,
And be a master of that ignorance
He outwardly professes, I am happy,
The pleasure I shall live in and the freedom
Without the squint-eye of the law upon me,
Or prating liberty of tongues, that envy.

ALTEA
You are a made woman.

MARGARITA
But if he should prove now
A crafty and dissembling kind of Husband,
One read in knavery, and brought up in the art
Of villany conceal'd.

ALTEA
My life, an innocent.

MARGARITA
That's it I aim at,
That's it I hope too, then I am sure I rule him,
For innocents are like obedient Children
Brought up under a hard Mother-in-law, a cruel,
Who being not us'd to break-fasts and collations,
When they have course bread offer'd 'em, are thankfull,
And take it for a favour too. Are the rooms
Made ready to entertain my friends? I long to dance now
And to be wanton; let me have a song, is the great couch up
The Duke of Medina sent?

ALTEA
'Tis up and ready.

MARGARITA
And day-beds in all chambers?

ALTEA
In all Lady,
Your house is nothing now but various pleasures,
The Gallants begin to gaze too.

MARGARITA
Let 'em gaze on,
I was brought up a Courtier, high and happy,
And company is my delight, and courtship,
And handsom servants at my will: where's my good husband,
Where does he wait?

ALTEA
He knows his distance Madam,
I warrant ye he is busie in the celler
Amongst his fellow servants, or asleep,
Till your command awake him.

[Enter **LEON**.

MARGARITA
'Tis well Altea.
It should be so, my ward I must preserve him.
Who sent for him, how dare he come uncall'd for,
His bonnet on too?

ALTEA
Sure he sees you not.

MARGARITA
How scornfully he looks!

LEON
Are all the chambers
Deckt and adorn'd thus for my Ladies pleasure?
New hangings every hour for entertainment,
And new plate bought, new Jewels to give lustre?

SERVANT
They are, and yet there must be more and richer,
It is her will.

LEON
Hum, is it so? 'tis excellent,
It is her will too, to have feasts and banquets,
Revells and masques.

SERVANT
She ever lov'd 'em dearly,
And we shall have the bravest house kept now Sir,
I must not call ye master she has warn'd me,
Nor must not put my hat off to ye.

LEON
'Tis no fashion,
What though I be her husband, I am your fellow,
I may cut first.

SERVANT
That's as you shall deserve Sir.

LEON
And when I lye with her.

SERVANT
May be I'le light ye,
On the same point you may doe me that service.

[Enter **FIRST LADY**.

FIRST LADY
Madam, the Duke Medina with some Captains
Will come to dinner, and have sent rare wine,
And their best services.

MARGARITA
They shall be welcom,
See all be ready in the noblest fashion,
The house perfum'd, now I shall take my pleasure,
And not my neighbour Justice maunder at me.
Go, get your best cloths on, but till I call ye,
Be sure you be not seen, dine with the Gentlewomen,
And behave your self cleanly Sir, 'tis for my credit.

[Enter **SECOND LADY**.

SECOND LADY
Madam, the Lady Julia.

LEON
That's a bawd,
A three pil'd bawd, bawd major to the army.

SECOND LADY
Has brought her coach to wait upon your Ladiship,
And to be inform'd if you will take the air this morning.

LEON
The neat air of her nunnery.

MARGARITA
Tell her no, i'th' afternoon I'le call on her.

SECOND LADY
I will Madam.

[Exit.

MARGARITA
Why are not you gone to prepare your self,
May be you shall be sewer to the fire course,
A portly presence, Altea he looks lean,
'Tis a wash knave, he will not keep his flesh well.

ALTEA
A willing, Madam, one that needs no spurring.

LEON
Faith madam, in my little understanding,
You had better entertain your honest neighbours,
Your friends about ye, that may speak well of ye,
And give a worthy mention of your bounty.

MARGARITA
How now, what's this?

LEON
'Tis only to perswade ye,
Courtiers are but tickle things to deal withal,
A kind of march-pane men that will not last Madam,
An egge and pepper goes farther than their potions,
And in a well built body, a poor parsnip
Will play his prize above their strong potabiles.

MARGARITA
The fellow's mad.

LEON
He that shall counsel Ladies,
That have both liquorish and ambitious eyes,
Is either mad, or drunk, let him speak Gospel.

ALTEA
He breaks out modestly.

LEON
Pray ye be not angry,
My indiscretion has made bold to tell ye,
What you'l find true.

MARGARITA
Thou darest not talk.

LEON
Not much Madam,
You have a tye upon your servants tongue,
He dares not be so bold as reason bids him,
'Twere fit there were a stronger on your temper.
Ne're look so stern upon me, I am your Husband,
But what are Husbands? read the new worlds wonders,
Such Husbands as this monstrous world produces,
And you will scarce find such deformities,
They are shadows to conceal your venial vertues,
Sails to your mills, that grind with all occasions,
Balls that lye by you, to wash out your stains,
And bills nail'd up with horn before your stories,
To rent out last.

MARGARITA
Do you hear him talk?

LEON
I have done Madam,
An oxe once spoke, as learned men deliver,
Shortly I shall be such, then I'le speak wonders,
Till when I tye my self to my obedience.

[Exit.

MARGARITA
First I'le unty my self, did you mark the Gentleman,
How boldly and how sawcily he talk'd,
And how unlike the lump I took him for,
The piece of ignorant dow, he stood up to me
And mated my commands, this was your providence,

Your wisdom, to elect this Gentleman,
Your excellent forecast in the man, your knowledge,
What think ye now?

ALTEA
I think him an Asse still,
This boldness some of your people have blown
Into him, this wisdom too with strong wine,
'Tis a Tyrant, and a Philosopher also, and finds
Out reasons.

MARGARITA
I'le have my celler lockt, no school kept there,
Nor no discovery. I'le turn my drunkards,
Such as are understanding in their draughts,
And dispute learnedly the whyes and wherefores,
To grass immediatly, I'le keep all fools,
Sober or drunk, still fools, that shall know nothing,
Nothing belongs to mankind, but obedience,
And such a hand I'le keep over this Husband.

ALTEA
He will fall again, my life he cryes by this time,
Keep him from drink, he has a high constitution.

[Enter **LEON**.

LEON
Shall I wear my new sute Madam?

MARGARITA
No your old clothes,
And get you into the country presently,
And see my hawks well train'd, you shall have victuals,
Such as are fit for sawcy palats Sir,
And lodgings with the hindes, it is too good too.

ALTEA
Good Madam be not so rough, with repentance,
You see now he's come round again.

MARGARITA
I see not what I expect to see.

LEON
You shall see Madam, if it shall please your Ladyship.

ALTEA

He's humbled,
Forgive good Lady,

MARGARITA
Well go get you handsom,
And let me hear no more.

LEON
Have ye yet no feeling?
I'le pinch ye to the bones then my proud Lady.

[Exit.

MARGARITA
See you preserve him thus upon my favour,
You know his temper, tye him to the grindstone,
The next rebellion I'le be rid of him,
I'le have no needy Rascals I tye to me,
Dispute my life: come in and see all handsom.

ALTEA
I hope to see you so too, I have wrought ill else.

[Exeunt.

[Enter **PEREZ**.

MICHAEL PEREZ
Shall I never return to mine own house again?
We are lodg'd here in the miserablest dog-hole,
A Conjurers circle gives content above it,
A hawks mew is a princely palace to it,
We have a bed no bigger than a basket,
And there we lie like butter clapt together,
And sweat our selves to sawce immediately,
The fumes are infinite inhabite here too;
And to that so thick, they cut like marmalet,
So various too, they'l pose a gold-finder,
Never return to mine own paradise?
Why wife I say, why Estifania.

ESTIFANIA
I am going presently.

MICHAEL PEREZ
Make haste good Jewel,
I am like the people that live in the sweet Islands:
I dye, I dye, if I stay but one day more here,

My lungs are rotten with the damps that rise,
And I cough nothing now but stinks of all sorts,
The inhabitants we have are two starv'd rats,
For they are not able to maintain a cat here,
And those appear as fearfull as two Devils,
They have eat a map of the whole world up already,
And if we stay a night we are gone for company.
There's an old woman that's now grown to marble,
Dri'd in this brick hill, and she sits i'th' chimnie,
Which is but three tiles rais'd like a house of cards,
The true proportion of an old smok'd Sibyl,
There is a young thing too that nature meant
For a maid-servant, but 'tis now a monster,
She has a husk about her like a chesnut
With basiness, and living under the line here,
And these two make a hollow sound together,
Like frogs or winds between two doors that murmur:

[Enter **ESTIFANIA**.

Mercy deliver me. O are you come wife,
Shall we be free again?

ESTIFANIA
I am now going,
And you shall presently to your own house Sir,
The remembrance of this small vexation
Will be argument of mirth for ever:
By that time you have said your orisons,
And broke your fast, I shall be back and ready,
To usher you to your old content, your freedom.

MICHAEL PEREZ
Break my neck rather, is there any thing here to eat
But one another, like a race of Cannibals?
A piece of butter'd wall you think is excellent,
Let's have our house again immediatly,
And pray ye take heed unto the furniture,
None be imbezil'd.

ESTIFANIA
Not a pin I warrant ye.

MICHAEL PEREZ
And let 'em instantly depart.

ESTIFANIA
They shall both,

There's reason in all courtesies, they must both,
For by this time I know she has acquainted him,
And has provided too, she sent me word Sir,
And will give over gratefully unto you.

MICHAEL PEREZ
I'le walk i'th' Church-yard,
The dead cannot offend more than these living,
An hour hence I'le expect ye.

ESTIFANIA
I'le not fail Sir.

MICHAEL PEREZ
And do you hear, let's have a handsom dinner,
And see all things be decent as they have been,
And let me have a strong bath to restore me,
I stink like a stal-fish shambles, or an oyl-shop.

ESTIFANIA
You shall have all, which some interpret nothing,
I'le send ye people for the trunks afore-hand,
And for the stuff.

MICHAEL PEREZ
Let 'em be known and honest,
And do my service to your niece.

ESTIFANIA
I shall Sir,
But if I come not at my hour, come thither,
That they may give you thanks for your fair courtesy,
And pray ye be brave for my sake.

MICHAEL PEREZ
I observe ye.

[Exeunt.

[Enter **JUAN DE CASTRO**, **SANCHO** and **CACAFOGO**.

SANCHIO
Thou art very brave.

CACAFOGO
I have reason, I have mony.

SANCHIO

Is mony reason?

CACAFOGO
Yes and rime too Captain,
If ye have no mony y'are an Asse.

SANCHIO
I thank ye.

CACAFOGO
Ye have manners, ever thank him that has mony.

SANCHIO
Wilt thou lend me any?

CACAFOGO
Not a farthing Captain,
Captains are casual things.

SANCHIO
Why so are all men, thou shalt have my bond.

CACAFOGO
Nor bonds nor fetters Captain,
My mony is mine, I make no doubt on't.

JUAN DE CASTRO
What dost thou do with it?

CACAFOGO
Put it to pious uses,
Buy Wine and Wenches, and undo young Coxcombs
That would undo me.

JUAN DE CASTRO
Are those Hospitals?

CACAFOGO
I first provide to fill my Hospitals
With Creatures of mine own, that I know wretched,
And then I build: those are more bound to pray for me:
Besides, I keep th' inheritance in my Name still.

JUAN DE CASTRO
A provident Charity; are you for the Wars, Sir?

CACAFOGO
I am not poor enough to be a Souldier,

Nor have I faith enough to ward a Bullet;
This is no lining for a trench, I take it.

JUAN DE CASTRO
Ye have said wisely.

CACAFOGO
Had you but my money,
You would swear it Colonel, I had rather drill at home
A hundred thousand Crowns, and with more honour,
Than exercise ten thousand Fools with nothing,
A wise Man safely feeds, Fools cut their fingers.

SANCHIO
A right State Usurer; why dost thou not marry,
And live a reverend Justice?

CACAFOGO
Is't not nobler to command a reverend Justice, than to be one?
And for a Wife, what need I marry, Captain,
When every courteous Fool that owes me money,
Owes me his Wife too, to appease my fury?

JUAN DE CASTRO
Wilt thou go to dinner with us?

CACAFOGO
I will go, and view the Pearl of Spain, the Orient
Fair One, the rich One too, and I will be respected,
I bear my Patent here, I will talk to her,
And when your Captain's Ships shall stand aloof,
And pick your Noses, I will pick the purse
Of her affection.

JUAN DE CASTRO
The Duke dines there to day too, the Duke of Medina.

CACAFOGO
Let the King dine there,
He owes me money, and so far's my Creature,
And certainly I may make bold with mine own, Captain?

SANCHIO
Thou wilt eat monstrously.

CACAFOGO
Like a true born Spaniard,
Eat as I were in England where the Beef grows,

And I will drink abundantly, and then
Talk ye as wantonly as Ovid did,
To stir the Intellectuals of the Ladies;
I learnt it of my Father's amorous Scrivener.

JUAN DE CASTRO
If we should play now, you must supply me.

CACAFOGO
You must pawn a Horse troop,
And then have at ye Colonel.

SANCHIO
Come, let's go:
This Rascal will make rare sport; how the Ladies
Will laugh at him?

JUAN DE CASTRO
If I light on him I'll make his Purse sweat too.

CACAFOGO
Will ye lead, Gentlemen?

[Exeunt.

[Enter **PEREZ**, an old **WOMAN** and **MAID**.

MICHAEL PEREZ
Nay, pray ye come out, and let me understand ye,
And tune your pipe a little higher, Lady;
I'll hold ye fast: rub, how came my Trunks open?
And my Goods gone, what Pick-lock Spirit?

OLD WOMAN
Ha, what would ye have?

MICHAEL PEREZ
My Goods again, how came my Trunks all open?

OLD WOMAN
Are your Trunks open?

MICHAEL PEREZ
Yes, and Cloaths gone,
And Chains, and Jewels: how she smells like hung Beef,
The Palsey, and Picklocks, fye, how she belches,
The Spirit of Garlick.

OLD WOMAN
Where's your Gentlewoman?
The young fair Woman?

MICHAEL PEREZ
What's that to my question?
She is my wife, and gone about my business.

MAID
Is she your Wife, Sir?

MICHAEL PEREZ
Yes Sir, is that wonder?
Is the name of Wife unknown here?

OLD WOMAN
Is she truly, truly your Wife?

MICHAEL PEREZ
I think so, for I married her;
It was no Vision sure!

MAID
She has the Keys, Sir.

MICHAEL PEREZ
I know she has, but who has all my goods, Spirit?

OLD WOMAN
If you be married to that Gentlewoman,
You are a wretched man, she has twenty Husbands.

MAID
She tells you true.

OLD WOMAN
And she has cozen'd all, Sir.

MICHAEL PEREZ
The Devil she has! I had a fair house with her,
That stands hard by, and furnisht royally.

OLD WOMAN
You are cozen'd too, 'tis none of hers, good Gentleman.

MAID
The Lady Margarita, she was her Servant,
And kept the house, but going from her, Sir,

For some lewd tricks she plaid.

MICHAEL PEREZ
Plague o' the Devil,
Am I i'th' full Meridian of my Wisedom
Cheated by a stale Quean! what kind of Lady
Is that that owes the House?

OLD WOMAN
A young sweet Lady.

MICHAEL PEREZ
Of a low stature?

OLD WOMAN
She is indeed but little, but she is wondrous fair.

MICHAEL PEREZ
I feel I am cozen'd;
Now I am sensible I am undone,
This is the very Woman sure, that Cousin
She told me would entreat but for four days,
To make the house hers; I am entreated sweetly.

MAID
When she went out this morning, that I saw, Sir,
She had two Women at the door attending,
And there she gave 'em things, and loaded 'em,
But what they were—I heard your Trunks to open,
If they be yours?

MICHAEL PEREZ
They were mine while they were laden,
But now they have cast their Calves, they are not worth
Owning: was she her Mistress say you?

OLD WOMAN
Her own Mistress, her very Mistress, Sir, and all you saw
About and in that house was hers.

MICHAEL PEREZ
No Plate, no Jewels, nor no Hangings?

MAID
Not a farthing, she is poor, Sir, a poor shifting thing.

MICHAEL PEREZ
No money?

OLD WOMAN

Abominable poor, as poor as we are,
Money as rare to her unless she steal it,
But for one civil Gown her Lady gave her,
She may go bare, good Gentlewoman.

MICHAEL PEREZ

I am mad now,
I think I am as poor as she, I am wide else,
One civil Sute I have left too, and that's all,
And if she steal that she must fley me for it;
Where does she use?

OLD WOMAN

You may find truth as soon,
Alas, a thousand conceal'd corners, Sir, she lurks in.
And here she gets a fleece, and there another,
And lives in mists and smoaks where none can find her.

MICHAEL PEREZ

Is she a Whore too?

OLD WOMAN

Little better, Gentleman, I dare not say she is so Sir, because
She is yours, Sir, these five years she has firkt
A pretty Living,
Until she came to serve; I fear he will knock my
Brains out for lying.

MICHAEL PEREZ

She has serv'd me faithfully,
A Whore and Thief? two excellent moral learnings
In one she-Saint, I hope to see her legend.
Have I been fear'd for my discoveries,
And courted by all Women to conceal 'em?
Have I so long studied the art of this Sex,
And read the warnings to young Gentlemen?
Have I profest to tame the Pride of Ladies,
And make 'em bear all tests, and am I trickt now?
Caught in mine own nooze? here's a royal left yet,
There's for your lodging and your meat for this Week.
A silk Worm lives at a more plentiful ordinary,
And sleeps in a sweeter Box: farewel great Grandmother,
If I do find you were an accessary,
'Tis but the cutting off too smoaky minutes,
I'll hang ye presently.

OLD WOMAN
And I deserve it, I tell but truth.

MICHAEL PEREZ
Not I, I am an Ass, Mother.

[Exeunt.

[Enter the **DUKE OF MEDINA, JUAN DE CASTRO, ALONZO, SANCHIO, CACAFOGO, ATTENDANTS**.

DUKE OF MEDINA
A goodly house.

JUAN DE CASTRO
And richly furnisht too, Sir.

ALONZO
Hung wantonly, I like that preparation,
It stirs the blood unto a hopeful Banquet,
And intimates the Mistress free and jovial,
I love a house where pleasure prepares welcome.

DUKE OF MEDINA
Now Cacafogo, how like you this mansion?
'Twere a brave Pawn.

CACAFOGO
I shall be master of it,
'Twas built for my bulk, the rooms are wide and spacious,
Airy and full of ease, and that I love well,
I'll tell you when I taste the Wine, my Lord,
And take the height of her Table with my Stomach,
How my affections stand to the young Lady.

[Enter **MARGARITA, ALTEA, LADIES** and **SERVANTS**.

MARGARITA
All welcome to your Grace, and to these Souldiers,
You honour my poor house with your fair presence,
Those few slight pleasures that inhabit here, Sir,
I do beseech your Grace command, they are yours,
Your servant but preserves 'em to delight ye.

DUKE OF MEDINA
I thank ye Lady, I am bold to visit ye,
Once more to bless mine eyes with your sweet Beauty,
'T has been a long night since you left the Court,
For till I saw you now, no day broke to me.

MARGARITA
Bring in the Dukes meat.

SANCHIO
She is most excellent.

JUAN DE CASTRO
Most admirable fair as e'r I look'd upon,
I had rather command her than my Regiment.

CACAFOGO
I'll have a fling, 'tis but a thousand Duckets,
Which I can cozen up again in ten days,
And some few Jewels to justifie my Knavery,
Say, I should marry her, she'll get more money
Than all my Usury, put my Knavery to it,
She appears the most infallible way of Purchase,
I you'd wish her a size or two stronger for the encounter,
For I am like a Lion where I lay hold,
But these Lambs will endure a plaguy load,
And never bleat neither, that Sir, time has taught us,
I am so vertuous now, I cannot speak to her,
The arrant'st shamefac'd Ass, I broil away too.

[Enter **LEON**.

MARGARITA
Why, where's this dinner?

LEON
'Tis not ready, Madam,
Nor shall not be until I know the Guests too,
Nor are they fairly welcome till I bid 'em.

JUAN DE CASTRO
Is not this my Alferes? he looks another thing;
Are miracles afoot again?

MARGARITA
Why, Sirrah, why Sirrah, you?

LEON
I hear you, saucy Woman,
And as you are my Wife, command your absence,
And know your duty, 'tis the Crown of modesty.

DUKE OF MEDINA

Your Wife?

LEON
Yes good my Lord, I am her Husband,
And pray take notice that I claim that honour,
And will maintain it.

CACAFOGO
It thou beest her Husband,
I am determin'd thou shalt be my Cuckold,
I'll be thy faithful friend.

LEON
Peace, dirt and dunghil,
I will not lose my anger on a Rascal,
Provoke me more, I'll beat thy blown body
Till thou rebound'st again like a Tennis-Ball.

ALONZO
This is miraculous.

SANCHIO
Is this the Fellow
That had the patience to become a Fool,
A flurted Fool, and on a sudden break,
As if he would shew a wonder to the World,
Both in Bravery, and Fortune too?
I much admire the man, I am astonisht.

MARGARITA
I'll be divorced immediately.

LEON
You shall not,
You shall not have so much will to be wicked.
I am more tender of your honour, Lady,
And of your Age, you took me for a shadow;
You took me to gloss over your discredit,
To be your Fool, you had thought you had found a Coxcomb;
I am innocent of any foul dishonour I mean to ye.
Only I will be known to be your Lord now,
And be a fair one too, or I will fall for't.

MARGARITA
I do command ye from me, thou poor fellow,
Thou cozen'd Fool.

LEON

Thou cozen'd Fool? 'tis not so,
I will not be commanded: I am above ye:
You may divorce me from your favour, Lady,
But from your state you never shall, I'll hold that,
And then maintain your wantonness, I'll wink at it.

MARGARITA
Am I braved thus in mine own house?

LEON
'Tis mine, Madam,
You are deceiv'd, I am Lord of it, I rule it and all that's in't;
You have nothing to do here, Madam;
But as a Servant to sweep clean the Lodgings,
And at my farther will to do me service,
And so I'll keep it.

MARGARITA
As you love me, give way.

LEON
It shall be better,
I will give none, Madam,
I stand upon the ground of mine own Honour,
And will maintain it, you shall know me now
To be an understanding feeling man,
And sensible of what a Woman aims at,
A young proud Woman that has Will to sail with,
An itching Woman, that her blood provokes too,
I cast my Cloud off, and appear my self,
The master of this little piece of mischief,
And I will put a Spell about your feet, Lady,
They shall not wander but where I give way now.

DUKE OF MEDINA
Is this the Fellow that the People pointed at,
For the meer sign of man, the walking Image?
He speaks wondrous highly.

LEON
As a Husband ought, Sir,
In his own house, and it becomes me well too,
I think your Grace would grieve if you were put to it
To have a Wife or Servant of your own,
(For Wives are reckon'd in the rank of Servants,)
Under your own roof to command ye.

JUAN DE CASTRO

Brave, a strange Conversion, thou shalt lead
In chief now.

DUKE OF MEDINA
Is there no difference betwixt her and you, Sir?

LEON
Not now, Lord, my Fortune makes me even,
And as I am an honest man, I am nobler.

MARGARITA
Get me my Coach.

LEON
Let me see who dares get it
Till I command, I'll make him draw your Coach too,
And eat your Coach, (which will be hard diet)
That executes your Will; or take your Coach, Lady,
I give you liberty, and take your People
Which I turn off, and take your Will abroad with ye,
Take all these freely, but take me no more,
And so farewel.

DUKE OF MEDINA
Nay, Sir, you shall not carry it
So bravely off, you shall not wrong a Lady
In a high huffing strain, and think to bear it,
We stand not by as Bawds to your brave fury,
To see a Lady weep.

LEON
They are tears of anger, I beseech ye note 'em, not worth pity,
Wrung from her rage, because her Will prevails not,
She would swound now if she could not cry,
Else they were excellent, and I should grieve too,
But falling thus, they show nor sweet nor orient.
Put up my Lord, this is oppression,
And calls the Sword of Justice to relieve me,
The law to lend her hand, the King to right me,
All which shall understand how you provoke me,
In mine own house to brave me, is this princely?
Then to my Guard, and if I spare your Grace,
And do not make this place your Monument,
Too rich a Tomb for such a rude behaviour,
I have a Cause will kill a thousand of ye, mercy forsake me.

JUAN DE CASTRO
Hold, fair Sir, I beseech ye,

The Gentleman but pleads his own right nobly.

LEON
He that dares strike against the husbands freedom,
The Husbands Curse stick to him, a tam'd Cuckold,
His Wife be fair and young, but most dishonest,
Most impudent, and have no feeling of it,
No conscience to reclaim her from a Monster,
Let her lye by him like a flattering ruine,
And at one instant kill both Name and Honour,
Let him be lost, no eye to weep his end,
Nor find no earth that's base enough to bury him.
Now Sir, fall on, I am ready to oppose ye.

DUKE OF MEDINA
I have better thought, I pray Sir use your Wife well.

LEON
Mine own humanity will teach me that, Sir,
And now you are all welcome, all, and we'll to dinner,
This is my Wedding-day.

DUKE OF MEDINA
I'll cross your joy yet.

JUAN DE CASTRO
I made seen a miracle, hold thine own, Souldier,
Sure they dare fight in fire that conquer Women.

SANCHIO
H'as beaten all my loose thoughts out of me,
As if he had thresht 'em out o'th' husk.

[Enter **PEREZ**.

MICHAEL PEREZ
'Save ye, which is the Lady of the house?

LEON
That's she, Sir, that pretty Lady,
If you would speak with her.

JUAN DE CASTRO
Don Michael, Leon, another darer come.

MICHAEL PEREZ
Pray do not know me, I am full of business,
When I have more time I'll be merry with ye.

It is the Woman: good Madam, tell me truly,
Had you a Maid call'd Estifania?

MARGARITA
Yes truly, had I.

MICHAEL PEREZ
Was she a Maid do you think?

MARGARITA
I dare not swear for her,
For she had but a scant Fame.

MICHAEL PEREZ
Was she your Kinswoman?

MARGARITA
Not that I ever knew, now I look better
I think you married her, 'give you joy, Sir,
You may reclaim her, 'twas a wild young Girl.

MICHAEL PEREZ
Give me a halter: is not this house mine, Madam?
Was not she owner of it, pray speak truly?

MARGARITA
No, certainly, I am sure my money paid for it,
And I ne'r remember yet I gave it you, Sir.

MICHAEL PEREZ
The Hangings and the Plate too?

MARGARITA
All are mine, Sir,
And every thing you see about the building,
She only kept my house when I was absent,
And so ill kept it, I was weary of her.

SANCHIO
What a Devil ails he?

JUAN DE CASTRO
He's possest I'll assure you.

MICHAEL PEREZ
Where is your Maid?

MARGARITA

Do not you know that have her?
She is yours now, why should I look after her?
Since that first hour I came I never saw her.

MICHAEL PEREZ
I saw her later, would the Devil had had her,
It is all true I find, a wild-fire take her.

JUAN DE CASTRO
Is thy Wife with Child, Don Michael? thy excellent wife.
Art thou a Man yet?

ALONZO
When shall we come and visit thee?

SANCHIO
And eat some rare fruit? thou hast admirable Orchards,
You are so jealous now, pox o' your jealousie,
How scurvily you look!

MICHAEL PEREZ
Prithee leave fooling,
I am in no humour now to fool and prattle,
Did she ne'r play the wag with you?

MARGARITA
Yes many times, so often that I was asham'd to keep her,
But I forgave her, Sir, in hope she would mend still,
And had not you o'th' instant married her,
I had put her off.

MICHAEL PEREZ
I thank ye, I am blest still,
Which way so e'r I turn I am a made man,
Miserably gull'd beyond recovery.

JUAN DE CASTRO
You'll stay and dine?

MICHAEL PEREZ
Certain I cannot, Captain,
Hark in thine ear, I am the arrantst Puppy,
The miserablest Ass, but I must leave ye,
I am in haste, in haste, bless you, good Madam,
And you prove as good as my Wife.

[Exit.

LEON
Will you come near, Sir, will your Grace but honour me,
And taste our dinner? you are nobly welcome,
All anger's past I hope, and I shall serve ye.

JUAN DE CASTRO
Thou art the stock of men, and I admire thee.

[Exeunt.

ACTUS QUARTUS

SCÆNA PRIMA

Enter **PEREZ**.

MICHAEL PEREZ
I'll go to a Conjurer but I'll find this Pol-cat,
This pilfering Whore: a plague of Vails, I cry,
And covers for the impudence of Women,
Their sanctity in show will deceive Devils,
It is my evil Angel, let me bless me.

[Enter **ESTIFANIA** with a Casket.

ESTIFANIA
'Tis he, I am caught, I must stand to it stoutly,
And show no shake of fear, I see he is angry,
Vext at the uttermost.

MICHAEL PEREZ
My worthy Wife,
I have been looking of your modesty
All the town over.

ESTIFANIA
My most noble Husband,
I am glad I have found ye, for in truth I am weary,
Weary and lame with looking out your Lordship.

MICHAEL PEREZ
I have been in Bawdy Houses.

ESTIFANIA
I believe you, and very lately too.

MICHAEL PEREZ
'Pray you pardon me,
To seek your Ladyship, I have been in Cellars,
In private Cellars, where the thirsty Bawds
Hear your Confessions; I have been at Plays,
To look you out amongst the youthful Actors,
At Puppet Shews, you are Mistress of the motions,
At Gossippings I hearkned after you,
But amongst those Confusions of lewd Tongues
There's no distinguishing beyond a Babel.
I was amongst the Nuns because you sing well,
But they say yours are Bawdy Songs, they mourn for ye,
And last I went to Church to seek you out,
'Tis so long since you were there, they have forgot you.

ESTIFANIA
You have had a pretty progress, I'll tell mine now:
To look you out, I went to twenty Taverns.

MICHAEL PEREZ
And are you sober?

ESTIFANIA
Yes, I reel not yet, Sir,
Where I saw twenty drunk, most of 'em Souldiers,
There I had great hope to find you disguis'd too.
From hence to th' dicing-house, there I found
Quarrels needless, and senceless,
Swords and Pots, and Candlesticks,
Tables and Stools, and all in one confusion,
And no man knew his Friend. I left this Chaos,
And to the Chirurgions went, he will'd me stay,
For says he learnedly, if he be tipled,
Twenty to one he whores, and then I hear of him,
If he be mad, he quarrels, then he comes too.
I sought ye where no safe thing would have ventur'd,
Amongst diseases, base and vile, vile Women,
For I remembred your old Roman axiom,
The more the danger, still the more the Honour.
Last, to your Confessor I came, who told me,
You were too proud to pray, and here I have found ye.

MICHAEL PEREZ
She bears up bravely, and the Rogue is witty,
But I shall dash it instantly to nothing.
Here leave we off our wanton languages,
And now conclude we in a sharper tongue.

ESTIFANIA
Why am I cozen'd?
Why am I abused?

MICHAEL PEREZ
Thou most vile, base, abominable—

ESTIFANIA
Captain.

MICHAEL PEREZ
Thou stinking, overstew'd, poor, pocky—

ESTIFANIA
Captain.

MICHAEL PEREZ
Do you echo me?

ESTIFANIA
Yes Sir, and go before ye,
And round about ye, why do you rail at me
For that that was your own sin, your own knavery?

MICHAEL PEREZ
And brave me too?

ESTIFANIA
You had best now draw your Sword, Captain!
Draw it upon a Woman, do, brave Captain,
Upon your Wife, Oh most renowned Captain.

MICHAEL PEREZ
A Plague upon thee, answer me directly;
Why didst thou marry me?

ESTIFANIA
To be my Husband;
I had thought you had had infinite, but I'm cozen'd.

MICHAEL PEREZ
Why didst thou flatter me, and shew me wonders?
A house and riches, when they are but shadows,
Shadows to me?

ESTIFANIA
Why did you work on me
(It was but my part to requite you, Sir)

With your strong Souldiers wit, and swore you would bring me
So much in Chains, so much in Jewels, Husband,
So much in right rich Cloaths?

MICHAEL PEREZ
Thou hast 'em, Rascal;
I gave 'em to thy hands, my trunks and all,
And thou hast open'd 'em, and sold my treasure.

ESTIFANIA
Sir, there's your treasure, sell it to a Tinker
To mend old Kettles, is this noble Usage?
Let all the World view here the Captain's treasure,
A Man would think now, these were worthy matters;
Here's a shooing-horn Chain gilt over, how it scenteth
Worse than the mouldy durty heel it served for:
And here's another of a lesser value,
So little I would shame to tye my Dog in't,
These are my joynture, blush and save a labour,
Or these else will blush for ye.

MICHAEL PEREZ
A fire subtle ye, are ye so crafty?

ESTIFANIA
Here's a goodly jewel,
Did not you win this at Goletta, Captain,
Or took it in the field from some brave Bashaw
How it sparkles like an old Ladies eyes,
And fills each room with light like a close Lanthorn!
This would do rarely in an Abbey Window,
To cozen Pilgrims.

MICHAEL PEREZ
Prithee leave prating.

ESTIFANIA
And here's a Chain of Whitings eyes for pearls,
A Muscle-monger would have made a better.

MICHAEL PEREZ
Nay, prithee wife, my Cloaths, my Cloaths.

ESTIFANIA
I'll tell ye,
Your Cloaths are parallels to these, all counterfeit.
Put these and them on, you are a Man of Copper,
A kind of Candlestick; these you thought, my Husband,

To have cozen'd me withall, but I am quit with you.

MICHAEL PEREZ
Is there no house then, nor no grounds about it?
No plate nor hangings?

ESTIFANIA
There are none, sweet Husband,
Shadow for shadow is as equal justice.
Can you rail now? pray put up your fury, Sir,
And speak great words, you are a Souldier, thunder.

MICHAEL PEREZ
I will speak little, I have plaid the Fool,
And so I am rewarded.

ESTIFANIA
You have spoke well, Sir,
And now I see you are so conformable
I'll heighten you again, go to your house,
They are packing to be gone, you must sup there,
I'll meet ye, and bring Cloaths, and clean Shirts after,
And all things shall be well, I'll colt you once more,
And teach you to bring Copper.

MICHAEL PEREZ
Tell me one thing,
I do beseech thee tell me, tell me truth, Wife,
However I forgive thee, art thou honest?
The Beldam swore.

ESTIFANIA
I bid her tell you so, Sir,
It was my plot, alas my credulous Husband,
The Lady told you too.

MICHAEL PEREZ
Most strange things of thee.

ESTIFANIA
Still 'twas my way, and all to try your sufferance,
And she denied the House.

MICHAEL PEREZ
She knew me not,
No, nor no title that I had.

ESTIFANIA

'Twas well carried;
No more, I am right and straight.

MICHAEL PEREZ
I would believe thee,
But Heaven knows how my heart is, will ye follow me?

ESTIFANIA
I'll be there straight.

MICHAEL PEREZ
I am fooled, yet dare not find it.

[Exit **PEREZ**.

ESTIFANIA
Go silly Fool, thou mayst be a good Souldier
In open field, but for our private service
Thou art an Ass, I'll make thee so, or miss else.

[Enter **CACAFOGO**.

Here comes another Trout that I must tickle,
And tickle daintily, I have lost my end else.
May I crave your leave, Sir?

CACAFOGO
Prithee be answered, thou shalt crave no leave,
I am in my meditations, do not vex me,
A beaten thing, but this hour a most bruised thing,
That people had compassion on it, looked so,
The next Sir Palmerin, here's fine proportion,
An Ass, and then an Elephant, sweet Justice,
There's no way left to come at her now, no craving,
If money could come near, yet I would pay him;
I have a mind to make him a huge Cuckold,
And money may do much, a thousand Duckets,
'Tis but the letting blood of a rank Heir.

ESTIFANIA
'Pray you hear me.

CACAFOGO
I know thou hast some wedding Ring to pawn now,
Of Silver and gilt, with a blind posie in't,
Love and a Mill-horse should go round together,
Or thy Childs whistle, or thy Squirrels Chain,
I'll none of 'em, I would she did but know me,

Or would this Fellow had but use of money,
That I might come in any way.

ESTIFANIA
I am gone, Sir,
And I shall tell the beauty sent me to ye,
The Lady Margarita.

CACAFOGO
Stay I prithee,
What is thy will? I turn me wholly to ye,
And talk now till thy tongue ake, I will hear ye.

ESTIFANIA
She would entreat you, Sir,

CACAFOGO
She shall command, Sir,
Let it be so, I beseech thee, my sweet Gentlewoman,
Do not forget thy self.

ESTIFANIA
She does command then
This courtesie, because she knows you are noble.

CACAFOGO
Your Mistress by the way?

ESTIFANIA
My natural mistress,
Upon these Jewels, Sir, they are fair and rich,
And view 'em right.

CACAFOGO
To doubt 'em is an heresie.

ESTIFANIA
A thousand Duckets, 'tis upon necessity
Of present use, her husband, Sir, is stubborn.

CACAFOGO
Long may he be so.

ESTIFANIA
She desires withal a better knowledge of your parts and person,
And when you please to do her so much honour.

CACAFOGO

Come, let's dispatch.

ESTIFANIA
In troth I have heard her say, Sir,
Of a fat man she has not seen a sweeter.
But in this business, Sir.

CACAFOGO
Let's do it first
And then dispute, the Ladies use may long for't.

ESTIFANIA
All secrecy she would desire, she told me
How wise you are.

CACAFOGO
We are not wise to talk thus,
Carry her the gold, I'le look her out a Jewel,
Shall sparkle like her eyes, and thee another,
Come prethee come, I long to serve thy Lady,
Long monstrously, now valor I shall meet ye,
You that dare Dukes.

ESTIFANIA
Green goose you are now in sippets.

[Exeunt.

[Enter the **DUKE OF MEDINA, SANCHIO, JUAN, ALONZO.**

DUKE OF MEDINA
He shall not have his will, I shall prevent him,
I have a toy here that will turn the tide,
And suddenly, and strangely, hear Don Juan,
Do you present it to him.

JUAN DE CASTRO
I am commanded.

[Exit.

DUKE OF MEDINA
A fellow founded out of Charity,
And moulded to the height contemn his maker,
Curb the free hand that fram'd him? This must not be.

SANCHIO
That such an oyster shell should hold a pearl,

And of so rare a price in prison,
Was she made to be the matter of her own undoing,
To let a slovenly unweildy fellow,
Unruly and self will'd, dispose her beauties?
We suffer all Sir in this sad Eclipse,
She should shine where she might show like her self,
An absolute sweetness, to comfort those admire her,
And shed her beams upon her friends.
We are gull'd all,
And all the world will grumble at your patience,
If she be ravish't thus.

DUKE OF MEDINA
Ne'r fear it Sanchio,
We'l have her free again, and move at Court
In her clear orb: but one sweet handsomeness,
To bless this part of Spain, and have that slubber'd?

ALONZO
'Tis every good mans cause, and we must stir in it.

DUKE OF MEDINA
I'le warrant he shall be glad to please us,
And glad to share too, we shall hear anon
A new song from him, let's attend a little.

[Exeunt.

[Enter **LEON** and **JUAN DE CASTRO** with a commission.

LEON
Coronel, I am bound to you for this nobleness,
I should have been your officer, 'tis true Sir,
And a proud man I should have been to have serv'd you,
'T has pleas'd the King out of his boundless favours,
To make me your companion, this commission
Gives me a troop of horse.

JUAN DE CASTRO
I do rejoyce at it,
And am a glad man we shall gain your company,
I am sure the King knows you are newly married,
And out of that respect gives you more time Sir.

LEON
Within four daies I am gone, so he commands me,
And 'tis not mannerly for me to argue it,
The time grows shorter still, are your goods ready?

JUAN DE CASTRO
They are aboard.

LEON
Who waits there?

[Enter **SERVANT**.

SERVANT
Sir.

LEON
Do you hear ho, go carry this unto your Mistris Sir,
And let her see how much the King has honour'd me,
Bid her be lusty, she must make a Souldier.

[Exit.

[Enter **LORENZO**.

LORENZO
Sir,
Go take down all the hangings,
And pack up all my cloths, my plate and Jewels,
And all the furniture that's portable,
Sir when we lye in garrison, 'tis necessary
We keep a handsom port, for the Kings honour;
And do you hear, let all your Ladies wardrobe
Be safely plac'd in trunks, they must along too.

LORENZO
Whither must they goe Sir?

LEON
To the wars, Lorenzo,
And you and all, I will not leave a turn-spit,
That has one dram of spleen against a Dutchman.

LORENZO
Why then St Jaques hey, you have made us all Sir,
And if we leave ye—does my Lady goe too?

LEON
The stuff must goe to morrow towards the sea Sir,
All, all must goe.

LORENZO

Why Pedro, Vasco, Dego,
Come help me, come come boys, soldadocs, comrades,
We'l fley these beer-bellied rogues, come away quickly.

[Exit.

JUAN DE CASTRO
H'as taken a brave way to save his honour,
And cross the Duke, now I shall love him dearly,
By the life of credit thou art a noble Gentleman.

[Enter **MARGARITA**, led by two **LADIES**.

LEON
Why how now wife, what, sick at my preferment?
This is not kindly done.

MARGARITA
No sooner love ye,
Love ye intirely Sir, brought to consider
The goodness of your mind and mine own duty,
But lose you instantly, be divorc'd from ye?
This is a cruelty, I'le to the King
And tell him 'tis unjust to part two souls,
Two minds so nearly mixt.

LEON
By no means sweet heart.

MARGARITA
If he were married but four daies as I am.

LEON
He would hang himself the fifth, or fly his Country.

MARGARITA
He would make it treason for that tongue that durst
But talk of war, or any thing to vex him,
You shall not goe.

LEON
Indeed I must sweet wife,
What shall I lose the King for a few kisses?
We'l have enough.

MARGARITA
I'le to the Duke my cousin, he shall to th' King.

LEON
He did me this great office,
I thank his grace for't, should I pray him now,
To undoe't again? fye 'twere a base discredit.

MARGARITA
Would I were able Sir to bear you company,
How willing should I be then, and how merry!
I will not live alone.

LEON
Be in peace, you shall not.

[Knock within.

MARGARITA
What knocking's this? oh Heaven my head, why rascals
I think the war's begun i'th' house already.

LEON
The preparation is, they are taking down,
And packing up the hangings, plate and Jewels,
And all those furnitures that shall befit me
When I lye in garrison.

[Enter **COACHMAN**.

COACHMAN
Must the Coach goe too Sir?

LEON
How will your Lady pass to th' sea else easily?
We shall find shipping for't there to transport it.

MARGARITA
I goe? alas!

LEON
I'le have a main care of ye,
I know ye are sickly, he shall drive the easier,
And all accommodation shall attend ye.

MARGARITA
Would I were able.

LEON
Come I warrant ye,
Am not I with ye sweet? are her cloaths packt up,

And all her linnen? give your maids direction,
You know my time's but short, and I am commanded.

MARGARITA
Let me have a nurse,
And all such necessary people with me,
And an easie bark.

LEON
It shall not trot I warrant ye,
Curvet it may sometimes.

MARGARITA
I am with child Sir.

LEON
At four days warning? this is something speedy,
Do you conceive as our jennets do with a west winde?
My heir will be an arrant fleet one Lady,
I'le swear you were a maid when I first lay with ye.

MARGARITA
Pray do not swear, I thought I was a maid too,
But we may both be cozen'd in that point Sir.

LEON
In such a strait point sure I could not err Madam.

JUAN DE CASTRO
This is another tenderness to try him,
Fetch her up now.

MARGARITA
You must provide a cradle, and what a troubles that?

LEON
The sea shall rock it,
'Tis the best nurse; 'twill roar and rock together,
A swinging storm will sing you such a lullaby.

MARGARITA
Faith let me stay, I shall but shame ye Sir.

LEON
And you were a thousand shames you shall along with me,
At home I am sure you'l prove a million,
Every man carries the bundle of his sins
Upon his own back, you are mine, I'le sweat for ye.

[Enter **DUKE OF MEDINA, ALONZO, SANCHIO**.

DUKE OF MEDINA
What Sir, preparing for your noble journey?
'Tis well, and full of care.
I saw your mind was wedded to the war,
And knew you would prove some good man for your country,
Therefore fair Cousin with your gentle pardon,
I got this place: what, mourn at his advancement?
You are to blame, he will come again sweet cousin,
Mean time like sad Penelope and sage,
Amongst your maids at home, and huswifely.

LEON
No Sir, I dare not leave her to that solitariness,
She is young, and grief or ill news from those quarters
May daily cross her, she shall goe along Sir.

DUKE OF MEDINA
By no means Captain.

LEON
By all means an't please ye.

DUKE OF MEDINA
What take a young and tender bodied Lady,
And expose her to those dangers, and those tumults,
A sickly Lady too?

LEON
'Twill make her well Sir,
There's no such friend to health as wholsom travel.

SANCHIO
Away it must not be.

ALONZO
It ought not Sir,
Go hurry her? it is not humane, Captain.

DUKE OF MEDINA
I cannot blame her tears, fright her with tempests,
With thunder of the war.
I dare swear if she were able.

LEON
She is most able.

And pray ye swear not, she must goe, there's no remedy,
Nor greatness, nor the trick you had to part us,
Which I smell too rank, too open, too evident
(And I must tell you Sir, 'tis most unnoble)
Shall hinder me: had she but ten hours life,
Nay less, but two hours, I would have her with me,
I would not leave her fame to so much ruine,
To such a desolation and discredit
As her weakness and your hot will wou'd work her to.

[Enter **PEREZ**.

What Masque is this now?
More tropes and figures, to abuse my sufferance,
What cousin's this?

JUAN DE CASTRO
Michael van owle, how dost thou?
In what dark barn or tod of aged Ivy
Hast thou lyen hid?

MICHAEL PEREZ
Things must both ebbe and flow, Coronel,
And people must conceal, and shine again.
You are welcom hither as your friend may say, Gentleman,
A pretty house ye see handsomely seated,
Sweet and convenient walks, the waters crystal.

ALONZO
He's certain mad.

JUAN DE CASTRO
As mad as a French Tayler,
That has nothing in's head but ends of fustians.

MICHAEL PEREZ
I see you are packing now my gentle cousin,
And my wife told me I should find it so,
'Tis true I do, you were merry when I was last here,
But 'twas your will to try my patience Madam.
I am sorry that my swift occasions
Can let you take your pleasure here no longer,
Yet I would have you think my honour'd cousin,
This house and all I have are all your servants.

LEON
What house, what pleasure Sir, what do you mean?

MICHAEL PEREZ
You hold the jest so stiff, 'twill prove discourteous,
This house I mean, the pleasures of this place.

LEON
And what of them?

MICHAEL PEREZ
They are mine Sir, and you know it,
My wifes I mean, and so confer'd upon me,
The hangings Sir I must entreat, your servants,
That are so busie in their offices,
Again to minister to their right uses,
I shall take view o'th' plate anon, and furnitures
That are of under place; you are merry still cousin,
And of a pleasant constitution,
Men of great fortunes make their mirths at placitum.

LEON
Prethee good stubborn wife, tell me directly,
Good evil wife leave fooling and tell me honestly,
Is this my kinsman?

MARGARITA
I can tell ye nothing.

LEON
I have many kinsmen, but so mad a one,
And so phantastick—all the house?

MICHAEL PEREZ
All mine,
And all within it. I will not bate ye an ace on't.
Can you not receive a noble courtesie,
And quietly and handsomely as ye ought Couz,
But you must ride o'th' top on't?

LEON
Canst thou fight?

MICHAEL PEREZ
I'le tell ye presently, I could have done Sir.

LEON
For ye must law and claw before ye get it.

JUAN DE CASTRO
Away, no quarrels.

LEON

Now I am more temperate,
I'le have it prov'd if you were never yet in Bedlam,
Never in love, for that's a lunacy,
No great state left ye that you never lookt for,
Nor cannot manage, that's a rank distemper;
That you were christen'd, and who answer'd for ye,
And then I yield.

MICHAEL PEREZ

H'as half perswaded me I was bred i'th' moon,
I have ne'r a bush at my breech, are not we both mad,
And is not this a phantastick house we are in,
And all a dream we do? will ye walk out Sir,
And if I do not beat thee presently
Into a sound belief, as sense can give thee,
Brick me into that wall there for a chimny piece,
And say I was one o'th' Caesars, done by a seal-cutter.

LEON

I'le talk no more, come we'l away immediatly.

MARGARITA

Why then the house is his, and all that's in it,
I'le give away my skin but I'le undoe ye,
I gave it to his wife, you must restore Sir,
And make a new provision.

MICHAEL PEREZ

Am I mad now or am I christen'd, you my pagan cousin,
My mighty Mahound kinsman, what quirk now?
You shall be welcom all, I hope to see Sir
Your Grace here, and my couz, we are all Souldiers,
And must do naturally for one another.

DUKE OF MEDINA

Are ye blank at this? then I must tell ye Sir,
Ye have no command, now ye may goe at pleasure
And ride your asse troop, 'twas a trick I us'd
To try your jealousie upon entreatie,
And saving of your wife.

LEON

All this not moves me,
Nor stirs my gall, nor alters my affections,
You have more furniture, more houses Lady,
And rich ones too, I will make bold with those,

And you have Land i'th' Indies as I take it,
Thither we'l goe, and view a while those climats,
Visit your Factors there, that may betray ye,
'Tis done, we must goe.

MARGARITA
Now thou art a brave Gentleman,
And by this sacred light I love thee dearly.
The house is none of yours, I did but jest Sir,
Nor you are no couz of mine, I beseech ye vanish,
I tell you plain, you have no more right than he
Has, that senseless thing, your wife has once more fool'd ye:
Goe ye and consider.

LEON
Good morrow my sweet cousin, I should be glad Sir.

MICHAEL PEREZ
By this hand she dies for't,
Or any man that speaks for her.

[Exit **PEREZ**.

JUAN DE CASTRO
These are fine toyes.

MARGARITA
Let me request you stay but one poor month,
You shall have a Commission and I'le goe too,
Give me but will so far.

LEON
Well I will try ye,
Good morrow to your Grace, we have private business.

DUKE OF MEDINA
If I miss thee again, I am an arrant bungler.

JUAN DE CASTRO
Thou shalt have my command, and I'le march under thee,
Nay be thy boy before thou shalt be baffled,
Thou art so brave a fellow.

ALONZO
I have seen visions.

[Exeunt.

SCÆNA PRIMA

Enter **LEON**, with a letter, and **MARGARITA**.

LEON
Come hither wife, do you know this hand?

MARGARITA
I do Sir,
'Tis Estifania, that was once my woman.

LEON
She writes to me here, that one Cacafogo
An usuring Jewellers son (I know the Rascal)
Is mortally faln in love with ye.

MARGARITA
Is a monster, deliver me from mountains.

LEON
Do you goe a birding for all sorts of people?
And this evening will come to ye and shew ye Jewels,
And offers any thing to get access to ye,
If I can make or sport or profit on him,
(For he is fit for both) she bids me use him,
And so I will, be you conformable, and follow but my will.

MARGARITA
I shall not fail, Sir.

LEON
Will the Duke come again do you think?

MARGARITA
No sure Sir,
H'as now no policie to bring him hither.

LEON
Nor bring you to him, if my wit hold fair wife:
Let's in to dinner.

[Exeunt.

[Enter **PEREZ**.

MICHAEL PEREZ
Had I but lungs enough to bawl sufficiently,
That all the queans in Christendom might hear me,
That men might run away from contagion,
I had my wish; would it were most high treason,
Most infinite high, for any man to marry,
I mean for any man that would live handsomely,
And like a Gentleman, in his wits and credit.
What torments shall I put her to, Phalaris bull now,
Pox they love bulling too well, though they smoak for't.
Cut her apieces? every piece will live still,
And every morsel of her will do mischief;
They have so many lives, there's no hanging of 'em,
They are too light to drown, they are cork and feathers;
To burn too cold, they live like Salamanders;
Under huge heaps of stones to bury her,
And so depress her as they did the Giants;
She will move under more than built old Babel,
I must destroy her.

[Enter **CACAFOGO**, with a Casket.

CACAFOGO
Be cozen'd by a thing of clouts, a she moth,
That every silkmans shop breeds; to be cheated,
And of a thousand duckets by a whim wham?

MICHAEL PEREZ
Who's that is cheated, speak again thou vision,
But art thou cheated? minister some comfort:
Tell me directly art thou cheated bravely?
Come, prethee come, art thou so pure a coxcomb
To be undone? do not dissemble with me,
Tell me I conjure thee.

CACAFOGO
Then keep thy circle,
For I am a spirit wild that flies about thee,
And who e're thou art, if thou be'st humane,
I'le let thee plainly know, I am cheated damnably.

MICHAEL PEREZ
Ha, ha, ha.

CACAFOGO
Dost thou laugh? damnably, I say most damnably.

MICHAEL PEREZ
By whom, good spirit speak, speak ha, ha, ha.

CACAFOGO
I will utter, laugh till thy lungs crack, by a rascal woman,
A lewd, abominable, and plain woman.
Dost thou laugh still?

MICHAEL PEREZ
I must laugh, prethee pardon me,
I shall laugh terribly.

CACAFOGO
I shall be angry, terrible angry, I have cause.

MICHAEL PEREZ
That's it, and 'tis no reason but thou shouldst be angry,
Angry at heart, yet I must laugh still at thee.
By a woman cheated? art' sure it was a woman?

CACAFOGO
I shall break thy head, my valour itches at thee.

MICHAEL PEREZ
It is no matter, by a woman cozen'd,
A real woman?

CACAFOGO
A real Devil,
Plague of her Jewels and her copper chains,
How rank they smell.

MICHAEL PEREZ
Sweet cozen'd Sir let me see them,
I have been cheated too, I would have you note that,
And lewdly cheated, by a woman also,
A scurvie woman, I am undone sweet Sir,
Therefore I must have leave to laugh.

CACAFOGO
Pray ye take it,
You are the merriest undone man in Europe.
What need we fiddles, bawdy songs and sack,
When our own miseries can make us merry?

MICHAEL PEREZ
Ha, ha, ha.
I have seen these Jewels, what a notable penniworth

Have you had next your heart? you will not take Sir
Some twenty Duckets?

CACAFOGO
Thou art deceiv'd, I will take.

MICHAEL PEREZ
To clear your bargain now.

CACAFOGO
I'le take some ten, some any thing, some half ten,
Half a Ducket.

MICHAEL PEREZ
An excellent lapidary set these stones sure,
Do you mark their waters?

CACAFOGO
Quick-sand choak their waters,
And hers that bought 'em too, but I shall find her.

MICHAEL PEREZ
And so shall I, I hope, but do not hurt her,
You cannot find in all this Kingdom,
(If you had need of cozening, as you may have,
For such gross natures will desire it often,
'Tis at some time too a fine variety,)
A woman that can cozen ye so neatly,
She has taken half mine anger off with this trick.

[Exit.

CACAFOGO
If I were valiant now, I would kill this fellow,
I have mony enough lies by me at a pinch
To pay for twenty Rascals lives that vex me,
I'le to this Lady, there I shall be satisfied.

[Exit.

[Enter **LEON** and **MARGARITA**.

LEON
Come, we'l away unto your country house,
And there we'l learn to live contently,
This place is full of charge, and full of hurry,
No part of sweetness dwells about these cities.

MARGARITA
Whither you will, I wait upon your pleasure;
Live in a hollow tree Sir, I'le live with ye.

LEON
I, now you strike a harmony, a true one,
When your obedience waits upon your Husband,
And your sick will aims at the care of honour,
Why now I dote upon ye, love ye dearly,
And my rough nature falls like roaring streams,
Clearly and sweetly into your embraces.
O what a Jewel is a woman excellent,
A wise, a vertuous and a noble woman!
When we meet such, we bear our stamps on both sides,
And through the world we hold our currant virtues,
Alone we are single medals, only faces,
And wear our fortunes out in useless shadows,
Command you now, and ease me of that trouble,
I'le be as humble to you as a servant,
Bid whom you please, invite your noble friends,
They shall be welcome all, visit acquaintance,
Goe at your pleasure, now experience
Has link't you fast unto the chain of goodness:
What noise is this, what dismal cry?

[Clashing swords. A cry within, down with their swords.

MARGARITA
'Tis loud too.
Sure there's some mischief done i'th' street, look out there.

LEON
Look out and help.

[Enter a **SERVANT**.

SERVANT
Oh Sir the Duke Medina.

LEON
What of the Duke Medina?

SERVANT
Oh sweet Gentleman, is almost slain.

MARGARITA
Away away and help him, all the house help.

[Exit **SERVANT**.

LEON
How slain? why Margarita,
Why wife, sure some new device they have a foot again,
Some trick upon my credit, I shall meet it,
I had rather guide a ship Imperial
Alone, and in a storm, than rule one woman.

[Enter **DUKE OF MEDINA, MARGARITA, SANCHIO, ALONZO, SERVANT**.

MARGARITA
How came ye hurt Sir?

DUKE OF MEDINA
I fell out with my friend the noble Coronel,
My cause was naught, for 'twas about your honour:
And he that wrongs the Innocent ne'r prospers,
And he has left me thus for charity,
Lend me a bed to ease my tortur'd body,
That e're I perish I may show my penitence,
I fear I am slain.

LEON
Help Gentlemen to carry him,
There shall be nothing in this house my Lord,
But as your own.

DUKE OF MEDINA
I thank ye noble Sir.

LEON
To bed with him, and wife give your attendance.

[Enter **JUAN DE CASTRO**.

JUAN DE CASTRO
Doctors and Surgions.

DUKE OF MEDINA
Do not disquiet me,
But let me take my leave in peace.

[Exit **DUKE OF MEDINA, SANCHIO, ALONZO, MARGARITA, SERVANT**.

LEON
Afore me
'Tis rarely counterfeited.

JUAN DE CASTRO

True, it is so Sir,
And take you heed, this last blow do not spoil ye,
He is not hurt, only we made a scuffle,
As though we purpos'd anger; that same scratch
On's hand he took, to colour all and draw compassion,
That he might get into your house more cunningly.
I must not stay, stand now, and y'are a brave fellow.

LEON

I thank ye noble Coronel, and I honour ye.

[Exit **JUAN DE CASTRO**.

Never be quiet?

[Enter **MARGARITA**.

MARGARITA

He's most desperate ill Sir,
I do not think these ten months will recover him.

LEON

Does he hire my house to play the fool in,
Or does it stand on Fairy ground, we are haunted,
Are all men and their wives troubled with dreams thus?

MARGARITA

What ail you Sir?

LEON

Nay what ail you sweet wife,
To put these daily pastimes on my patience?
What dost thou see in me, that I should suffer thus,
Have not I done my part like a true Husband,
And paid some desperate debts you never look'd for?

MARGARITA

You have done handsomely I must confess Sir.

LEON

Have I not kept thee waking like a hawk?
And watcht thee with delights to satisfy thee?
The very tithes of which had won a Widow.

MARGARITA

Alas I pity ye.

LEON
Thou wilt make me angry,
Thou never saw'st me mad yet.

MARGARITA
You are alwaies,
You carry a kind of bedlam still about ye.

LEON
If thou pursuest me further I run stark mad,
If you have more hurt Dukes or Gentlemen,
To lye here on your cure, I shall be desperate,
I know the trick, and you shall feel I know it,
Are ye so hot that no hedge can contain ye?
I'le have thee let blood in all the veins about thee,
I'le have thy thoughts found too, and have them open'd,
Thy spirits purg'd, for those are they that fire ye,
Thy maid shall be thy Mistris, thou the maid,
And all those servile labours that she reach at,
And goe through cheerfully, or else sleep empty,
That maid shall lye by me to teach you duty,
You in a pallet by to humble ye,
And grieve for what you lose.

MARGARITA
I have lost my self Sir,
And all that was my base self, disobedience,

[Kneels.

My wantonness, my stubborness I have lost too,
And now by that pure faith good wives are crown'd with,
By your own nobleness.

[Enter **ALTEA**.

LEON
I take ye up, and wear ye next my heart,
See you be worth it. Now what with you?

ALTEA
I come to tell my Lady,
There is a fulsome fellow would fain speak with her.

LEON
'Tis Cacafogo, goe and entertain him,
And draw him on with hopes.

MARGARITA

I shall observe ye.

LEON

I have a rare design upon that Gentleman,
And you must work too.

ALTEA

I shall Sir most willingly.

LEON

Away then both, and keep him close in some place
From the Dukes sight, and keep the Duke in too,
Make 'em believe both, I'le find time to cure 'em.

[Exeunt.

[Enter **PEREZ** and **ESTIFANIA**, with a Pistol, and a Dagger.

MICHAEL PEREZ

Why how darst thou meet me again thou rebel,
And knowst how thou hast used me thrice, thou rascal?
Were there not waies enough to fly my vengeance,
No holes nor vaults to hide thee from my fury,
But thou must meet me face to face to kill thee?
I would not seek thee to destroy thee willingly,
But now thou comest to invite me,
And comest upon me,
How like a sheep-biting Rogue taken i'th' manner,
And ready for the halter dost thou look now!
Thou hast a hanging look thou scurvy thing, hast ne'r a knife
Nor ever a string to lead thee to Elysium?
Be there no pitifull 'Pothecaries in this town,
That have compassion upon wretched women,
And dare administer a dram of rats-bane,
But thou must fall to me?

ESTIFANIA

I know you have mercy.

MICHAEL PEREZ

If I had tuns of mercy thou deserv'st none,
What new trick is now afoot, and what new houses
Have you i'th' air, what orchards in apparition,
What canst thou say for thy life?

ESTIFANIA

Little or nothing,
I know you'l kill me, and I know 'tis useless
To beg for mercy, pray let me draw my book out,
And pray a little.

MICHAEL PEREZ
Do, a very little,
For I have farther business than thy killing,
I have mony yet to borrow, speak when you are ready.

ESTIFANIA
Now now Sir, now,

[Shews a Pistol.

Come on, do you start off from me,
Do you swear great Captain, have you seen a spirit?

MICHAEL PEREZ
Do you wear guns?

ESTIFANIA
I am a Souldiers wife Sir,
And by that priviledge I may be arm'd,
Now what's the news, and let's discourse more friendly,
And talk of our affairs in peace.

MICHAEL PEREZ
Let me see,
Prethee let me see thy gun, 'tis a very pretty one.

ESTIFANIA
No no Sir, you shall feel.

MICHAEL PEREZ
Hold ye villain, what thine own Husband?

ESTIFANIA
Let mine own Husband then
Be in's own wits, there, there's a thousand duckets,
Who must provide for you, and yet you'l kill me.

MICHAEL PEREZ
I will not hurt thee for ten thousand millions.

ESTIFANIA
When will you redeem your Jewels, I have pawn'd 'em,
You see for what, we must keep touch.

MICHAEL PEREZ
I'le kiss thee,
And get as many more, I'le make thee famous,
Had we the house now!

ESTIFANIA
Come along with me,
If that be vanish't there be more to hire Sir.

MICHAEL PEREZ
I see I am an asse when thou art near me.

[Enter **LEON**, **MARGARITA** and **ALTEA** with a Taper.

LEON
Is the fool come?

ALTEA
Yes and i'th' celler fast,
And there he staies his good hour till I call him,
He will make dainty musick among the sack-butts,
I have put him just, Sir, under the Dukes chamber.

LEON
It is the better.

ALTEA
Has given me royally,
And to my Lady a whole load of portigues.

LEON
Better and better still, go Margarita,
Now play your prize, you say you dare be honest,
I'le put ye to your best.

MARGARITA
Secure your self Sir, give me the candle,
Pass away in silence.

[Exit **LEON** and **ALTEA**. She knocks.

DUKE OF MEDINA
Who's there, oh oh.

MARGARITA
My Lord,

DUKE OF MEDINA
Have ye brought me comfort?

MARGARITA
I have my Lord.
Come forth 'tis I, come gently out I'le help ye,

[Enter **DUKE OF MEDINA**, in a gown.

Come softly too, how do you?

DUKE OF MEDINA
Are there none here?
Let me look round; we cannot be too wary,

[Noise below.

Oh let me bless this hour, are you alone sweet friend?

MARGARITA
Alone to comfort you.
Cacafogo makes a noise below.

DUKE OF MEDINA
What's that you tumble?
I have heard a noise this half hour under me,
A fearfull noise.

MARGARITA
The fat thing's mad i'th' celler,
And stumbles from one hogs-head to another,
Two cups more, and he ne'r shall find the way out.
What do you fear? come, sit down by me chearfully,
My Husband's safe, how do your wounds?

DUKE OF MEDINA
I have none Lady,
My wounds I counterfeited cunningly,

[Noise below.

And feign'd the quarrel too, to injoy you sweet,
Let's lose no time, heark the same noise again.

MARGARITA
What noise, why look ye pale? I hear no stirring,
This goblin in the vault will be so tipled.
You are not well I know by your flying fancy,

Your body's ill at ease, your wounds.

DUKE OF MEDINA
I have none, I am as lusty and as full of health,
High in my blood.

MARGARITA
Weak in your blood you would say,
How wretched is my case, willing to please ye,
And find you so disable?

DUKE OF MEDINA
Believe me Lady.

MARGARITA
I know you will venture all you have to satisfy me,
Your life I know, but is it fit I spoil ye,
Is it my love do you think?

CACAFOGO
Here's to the Duke.

DUKE OF MEDINA
It nam'd me certainly,
I heard it plainly sound.

MARGARITA
You are hurt mortally,
And fitter for your prayers Sir than pleasure,
What starts you make? I would not kiss you wantonly,
For the world's wealth; have I secur'd my Husband,
And put all doubts aside to be deluded?

CACAFOGO
I come, I come.

DUKE OF MEDINA
Heaven bless me.

MARGARITA
And bless us both, for sure this is the Devil,
I plainly heard it now, he will come to fetch ye,
A very spirit, for he spoke under ground,
And spoke to you just as you would have snatcht me,
You are a wicked man, and sure this haunts ye,
Would you were out o'th' house.

DUKE OF MEDINA

I would I were,
O' that condition I had leapt a window.

MARGARITA
And that's the least leap if you mean to scape Sir,
Why what a frantick man were you to come here,
What a weak man to counterfeit deep wounds,
To wound another deeper!

DUKE OF MEDINA
Are you honest then?

MARGARITA
Yes then and now, and ever, and excellent honest,
And exercise this pastime but to shew ye,
Great men are fools sometimes as well as wretches.
Would you were well hurt, with any hope of life,
Cut to the brains, or run clean through the body,
To get out quietly as you got in Sir,
I wish it like a friend that loves ye dearly,
For if my Husband take ye, and take ye thus a counterfeit,
One that would clip his credit out of his honour,
He must kill ye presently,
There is no mercy nor an hour of pity,
And for me to intreat in such an agony,
Would shew me little better than one guilty,
Have you any mind to a Lady now?

DUKE OF MEDINA
Would I were off fair,
If ever Lady caught me in a trap more.

MARGARITA
If you be well and lusty, fy fy shake not,
You say you love me, come, come bravely now,
Despise all danger, I am ready for ye.

DUKE OF MEDINA
She mocks my misery, thou cruel Lady.

MARGARITA
Thou cruel Lord, wouldst thou betray my honesty,
Betray it in mine own house, wrong my Husband,
Like a night thief, thou darst not name by day-light?

DUKE OF MEDINA
I am most miserable.

MARGARITA

You are indeed,
And like a foolish thing you have made your self so,
Could not your own discretion tell ye Sir,
When I was married I was none of yours?
Your eyes were then commanded to look off me,
And I now stand in a circle and secure,
Your spells nor power can never reach my body,
Mark me but this, and then Sir be most miserable,
'Tis sacriledge to violate a wedlock,
You rob two Temples, make your self twice guilty,
You ruine hers, and spot her noble Husbands.

DUKE OF MEDINA

Let me be gone, I'le never more attempt ye.

MARGARITA

You cannot goe, 'tis not in me to save ye,
Dare ye do ill, and poorly then shrink under it?
Were I the Duke Medina, I would fight now,
For you must fight and bravely, it concerns you,
You do me double wrong if you sneak off Sir,
And all the world would say I lov'd a coward,
And you must dye too, for you will be kill'd,
And leave your youth, your honour and your state,
And all those dear delights you worship't here.

[Noise below.

DUKE OF MEDINA

The noise again!

CACAFOGO

Some small beer if you love me.

MARGARITA

The Devil haunts you sure, your sins are mighty.
A drunken Devil too, to plague your villany.

DUKE OF MEDINA

Preserve me but this once.

MARGARITA

There's a deep well
In the next yard, if you dare venture drowning,
It is but death.

DUKE OF MEDINA

I would not dye so wretchedly.

MARGARITA
Out of a garret window I'le let you down then,
But say the rope be rotten, 'tis huge high too.

DUKE OF MEDINA
Have you no mercy?

MARGARITA
Now you are frighted throughly,
And find what 'tis to play the fool in folly,
And see with clear eyes your detested folly,
I'le be your guard.

DUKE OF MEDINA
And I'le be your true servant,
Ever from this hour vertuously to love ye,
Chastly and modestly to look upon ye,
And here I seal it.

MARGARITA
I may kiss a stranger, for you must now be so.

[Enter **LEON, JUAN DE CASTRO, ALONZO, SANCHIO.**

LEON
How do you my Lord,
Me thinks you look but poorly on this matter.
Has my wife wounded ye, you were well before,
Pray Sir be comforted, I have forgot all,
Truly forgiven too, wife you are a right one,
And now with unknown nations I dare trust ye.

JUAN DE CASTRO
No more feign'd fights my Lord, they never prosper.

LEON
Who's this? the Devil in the vault?

ALTEA
'Tis he Sir, and as lovingly drunk, as though he had studied it.

CACAFOGO
Give me a cup of Sack, and kiss me Lady,
Kiss my sweet face, and make thy Husband cuckold,
An Ocean of sweet Sack, shall we speak treason?

LEON
He is Devilish drunk.

DUKE OF MEDINA
I had thought he had been a Devil.
He made as many noises and as horrible.

LEON
Oh a true lover Sir will lament loudly,
Which of the butts is your Mistris?

CACAFOGO
Butt in thy belly.

LEON
There's two in thine I am sure, 'tis grown so monstrous.

CACAFOGO
Butt in thy face.

LEON
Go carry him to sleep,
A fools love should be drunk, he has paid well for't too.
When he is sober let him out to rail,
Or hang himself, there will be no loss of him.

[Exit **CACAFOGO** and **SERVANT**.

[Enter **PEREZ**, and **ESTIFANIA**.

LEON
Who's this? my Mauhound cousin?

MICHAEL PEREZ
Good Sir, 'tis very good, would I had a house too,
For there is no talking in the open air,
My Tarmogant Couz, I would be bold to tell ye,
I durst be merry too; I tell you plainly,
You have a pretty seat, you have the luck on't,
A pretty Lady too, I have mist both,
My Carpenter built in a mist I thank him,
Do me the courtesie to let me see it,
See it but once more. But I shall cry for anger.
I'le hire a Chandlers shop close under ye,
And for my foolerie, sell sope and whip-cord,
Nay if you do not laugh now and laugh heartily,
You are a fool couz.

LEON
I must laugh a little,
And now I have done, couz thou shalt live with me,
My merry couz, the world shall not divorce us,
Thou art a valiant man, and thou shalt never want,
Will this content thee?

MICHAEL PEREZ
I'le cry, and then I'le be thankfull,
Indeed I will, and I'le be honest to ye.
I would live a swallow here I must confess.
Wife I forgive thee all if thou be honest,
At thy peril, I believe thee excellent.

ESTIFANIA
If I prove otherwaies, let me beg first,
Hold, this is yours, some recompence for service,
Use it to nobler ends than he that gave it.

DUKE OF MEDINA
And this is yours, your true commission, Sir,
Now you are a Captain.

LEON
You are a noble Prince Sir,
And now a souldier, Gentleman, we all rejoyce in't.

JUAN DE CASTRO
Sir, I shall wait upon you through all fortunes.

ALONZO
And I.

ALTEA
And I must needs attend my Mistris.

LEON
Will you goe Sister?

ALTEA
Yes indeed good Brother,
I have two ties, mine own bloud,
And my Mistris.

MARGARITA
Is she your Sister?

LEON

Yes indeed good wife,
And my best Sister,
For she prov'd so, wench,
When she deceiv'd you with a loving Husband.

ALTEA
I would not deal so truly for a stranger.

MARGARITA
Well I could chide ye,
But it must be lovingly and like a Sister,
I'le bring you on your way, and feast ye nobly,
For now I have an honest heart to love ye,
And then deliver you to the blue Neptune.

JUAN DE CASTRO
Your colours you must wear, and wear 'em proudly,
Wear 'em before the bullet, and in bloud too,
And all the world shall know
We are Vertues servants.

DUKE OF MEDINA
And all the world shall know, a noble mind
Makes women beautifull, and envie blind.

[Exeunt.

EPILOGUE

Good night our worthy friends, and may you part
Each with as merry and as free a heart
As you came hither; to those noble eyes
That deign to smile on our poor faculties,
And give a blessing to our labouring ends,
As we hope many, to such fortune sends
Their own desires, wives fair as light as chast;
To those that live by spight Wives made in hast.

John Fletcher – A Short Biography

John Fletcher was born in December, 1579 in Rye, Sussex. He was baptised on December 20th.

As can be imagined details of much of his life and career have not survived and, accordingly, only a very brief indication of his life and works can be given.

His father, Richard Fletcher, was a successful and rather ambitious cleric. From being the Dean of Peterborough he moved on to become the Bishop of Bristol, Bishop of Worcester and finally, shortly before his death, the Bishop of London. He was also the chaplain to Queen Elizabeth.

When he was Dean of Peterborough, Richard Fletcher, witnessed the execution of Mary, Queen of Scots. It was said he "knelt down on the scaffold steps and started to pray out loud and at length, in a prolonged and rhetorical style, as though determined to force his way into the pages of history". He cried out at her death, "So perish all the Queen's enemies!" All very dramatic but the family did have strong links to the Arts.

Young Fletcher appears at the very young age of eleven to have entered Corpus Christi College at Cambridge University in 1591. There are no records that he ever took a degree but there is some small evidence that he was being prepared for a career in the church.

However what is clear is that this was soon abandoned as he joined the stream of people who would leave University and decamp to the more bohemian life of commercial theatre in London.

Unfortunately his father fell out with Queen Elizabeth but appears to have been on his way to rehabilitation before his death in 1596. At his death he was, however, mired in debt.

The upbringing of the now teenage Fletcher and his seven siblings now passed to his paternal uncle, the poet and minor official Giles Fletcher. Giles, who had the patronage of the Earl of Essex may have been a liability rather than an advantage to the young Fletcher. With Essex involved in the failed rebellion against Elizabeth Giles was also tainted by association.

By 1606 John Fletcher appears to have equipped himself with the talents to become a playwright. Initially this appears to have been for the Children of the Queen's Revels, then performing at the Blackfriars Theatre.

Commendatory verses by Richard Brome in the Beaumont and Fletcher 1647 folio place Fletcher in the company of Ben Jonson, although it is not known when this friendship began. Jonson, of course, was a leviathan of English Literature, so admired that many of his literary friends and colleagues were simply known as 'Sons of Ben'. Fletcher's frequent early collaborator, Francis Beaumont, was also a friend of Jonson's.

Fletcher's early career was marked by one significant failure; The Faithful Shepherdess, his adaptation of Giovanni Battista Guarini's Il Pastor Fido, which was performed by the Blackfriars Children in 1608. In the preface to the printed edition of his play, Fletcher explained the failure as due to his audience's faulty expectations. They expected a pastoral tragicomedy to feature dances, comedy, and murder, with the shepherds presented in conventional stereotypes – as Fletcher put it, wearing "gray cloaks, with curtailed dogs in strings." Fletcher's preface is however best known for its pithy definition of tragicomedy: "A tragicomedy is not so called in respect of mirth and killing, but in respect it wants [i.e., lacks] deaths, which is enough to make it no tragedy; yet brings some near it, which is enough to make it no comedy." A comedy, he went on to say, must be "a representation of familiar people." His preface is critical of drama that features characters whose action violates nature.

In that case, Fletcher appears to have been developing a new style faster than audiences could comprehend. By 1609, however, he had found his stride. With Beaumont, he wrote Philaster, which became a hit for the King's Men and began a profitable association between Fletcher and that company. Philaster appears also to have begun a trend for tragicomedy. Fletcher's influence has also been said to have inspired some features of Shakespeare's late romances, and certainly his influence on the tragicomic work of other playwrights is even more marked.

By the middle of the 1610s, Fletcher's plays had achieved a popularity that rivalled Shakespeare's and cemented the pre-eminence of the King's Men in Jacobean London. After Beaumont's retirement, necessitated by ill-health, and then his early death in 1616, Fletcher continued working, both singly and in collaboration, until his death in 1625. By that time, he had produced, or had been credited with, close to fifty plays. This body of work remained a major part of the King's Men's repertory until the closing of the theatres in 1642 due to the Civil War.

At the beginning of his career Fletcher's most important collaborator was Francis Beaumont. The two wrote together for close to a decade, first for the Children of the Queen's Revels, and then for the King's Men. According to an anecdote transmitted or invented by John Aubrey, they also lived together in Bankside, sharing clothes and having "one wench in the house between them." This domestic arrangement, if it existed, was ended by Beaumont's marriage in 1613, and their dramatic partnership ended after Beaumont fell ill, probably of a stroke, that same year.

At this point Fletcher had written many plays with Beaumont and several others on his own. He seems to have been regarded as quite a talent although it should be remembered that playwrights were required to be prolific, to easily work with other collaborators and to produce work of quality and commercial appeal very quickly.

The King's Men, run by Philip Henslowe, was the most prestigious of the theatre companies and Fletcher now had an increasingly close association with it.

Fletcher collaborated with Shakespeare on Henry VIII, The Two Noble Kinsmen, and the now lost Cardenio, which some scholars say was the basis for Lewis Theobald's play Double Falsehood. (Theobald is regarded as one of the best Shakespearean editors. Whether his play is based on Cardenio or on some other is not absolutely known although Theobald certainly promoted it as his revision of the lost Shakespeare/Fletcher play.)

A play that Fletcher also wrote by himself at this time, The Woman's Prize or the Tamer Tamed, is also regarded as a sequel to The Taming of the Shrew.

In 1616, with the death of Shakespeare, Fletcher now appears to have entered into an enhanced arrangement with the King's Men on very similar terms to Shakespeare's. Fletcher would now write exclusively for the King's Men until his own death almost a decade later.

As well as continuing his solo productions Fletcher was still collaborating with other playwrights, mainly Philip Massinger, who, in turn, would succeed him as the in-house playwright for the King's Men.

Fletcher's popularity continued throughout his life; indeed during the winter of 1621, he had three of his plays performed at court. His mastery is most notable in two dramatic types; tragicomedy and the comedy of manners.

John Fletcher died in 1625, it is thought of bubonic plague which, at the time, was undergoing further outbreaks.

He seems to have been buried in what is now Southwark Cathedral, although a precise location is not known. There is much made of an anecdote that Fletcher and Massinger (who died in 1640) share the same grave but it is more likely that both are buried within a few yards of each other and that the stone markers in the floor have confused the issue. One is marked 'Edmond Shakespeare 1607' and the other 'John Fletcher 1625' refers to Shakespeare's younger brother and the playwright. The churchyards were, more often than not, completely over-crowded and breeding grounds for disease. Precise record keeping was not a practiced skill.

During the later Commonwealth, many of the playwright's best-known scenes were kept alive as drolls. These were brief performances, usually condensed into one or two scenes and with the addition of music or song to satisfy the taste for plays while the theatres were closed under the Puritans. At the re-opening of the theatres in 1660, the plays in the Fletcher canon, in original form or revised, were by far the most common productions on the English stage. The most frequently revived plays suggest the developing taste for comedies of manners. Among the tragedies, The Maid's Tragedy and, especially, Rollo Duke of Normandy held the stage. Four tragicomedies (A King and No King, The Humorous Lieutenant, Philaster, and The Island Princess) were popular, perhaps in part for their similarity to and foreshadowing of heroic drama. Four comedies (Rule a Wife And Have a Wife, The Chances, Beggars' Bush, and especially The Scornful Lady) were also stage mainstays.

Despite his popularity, and it appears he was held in higher regard than Shakespeare at this time, his works steadily lost ground to those of Shakespeare and to new productions from other playwrights.

Since then Fletcher has increasingly become a subject only for occasional revivals and for specialists. Fletcher and his collaborators have been the subject of important bibliographic and critical studies, but the plays have been revived only infrequently.

Due to the frequent collaborations between all manner of playwrights, and the revisions carried out in later years, having a settled list of authorship to any given set of plays can be problematic. The works of Fletcher and others of this period most definitely fall into this category. It is as well to take into account that during this period theatres were quite often closed either due to outbreaks of the plague or to the prevailing political and moral climate. Printers, anxious to provide materials that would sell, were not above changing a name or two to enhance sales.

Although Fletcher collaborated most often with Beaumont and Massinger, it is believed that Massinger revised many of the plays some time after their original production. Other collaborators including Nathan Field, William Shakespeare, William Rowley and others also can be seen distinctly in Fletchers' works. Many modern scholars point out that Fletcher had many particular mannerisms but other playwrights would also duplicate these at times so allocating exact contributions of anyone to a play is somewhat of a detective case in many instances. However from the original folio printings or licensing via the Master of the Revels (the statutory licensing authority to approve and censor plays as well a hand in publication and printing of theatrical materials) as well as contemporary notes a fairly precise bibliography of the works can be given with only a few plays lacking substantial authority and provenance.

This bibliography gives the most likely date of writing together with when published, revised or licensed by the Master or the Revels (This position within the royal household was originally for royal festivities, ie revels, and later to oversee stage censorship, until this function was transferred to the Lord Chamberlain in 1624).

Solo Plays

The Faithful Shepherdess, pastoral (written 1608–9; printed 1609)
The Tragedy of Valentinian, tragedy (1610–14; 1647)
Monsieur Thomas, comedy (c. 1610–16; 1639)
The Woman's Prize, or The Tamer Tamed, comedy (c. 1611; 1647)
Bonduca, tragedy (1611–14; 1647)
The Chances, comedy (c. 1613–25; 1647)
Wit Without Money, comedy (c. 1614; 1639)
The Mad Lover, tragicomedy (acted 5 January 1617; 1647)
The Loyal Subject, tragicomedy (licensed 16 November 1618; revised 1633; 1647)
The Humorous Lieutenant, tragicomedy (c. 1619; 1647)
Women Pleased, tragicomedy (c. 1619–23; 1647)
The Island Princess, tragicomedy (c. 1620; 1647)
The Wild Goose Chase, comedy (c. 1621; 1652)
The Pilgrim, comedy (c. 1621; 1647)
A Wife for a Month, tragicomedy (licensed 27 May 1624; 1647)
Rule a Wife and Have a Wife, comedy (licensed 19 October 1624; 1640)

Collaborations

With Francis Beaumont

The Woman Hater, comedy (1606; 1607)
Cupid's Revenge, tragedy (c. 1607–12; 1615)
Philaster, or Love Lies a-Bleeding, tragicomedy (c. 1609; 1620)
The Maid's Tragedy, Tragedy (c. 1609; 1619)
A King and No King, tragicomedy (1611; 1619)
The Captain, comedy (c. 1609–12; 1647)
The Scornful Lady, comedy (c. 1613; 1616)
Love's Pilgrimage, tragicomedy (c. 1615–16; 1647)
The Noble Gentleman, comedy (c. 1613; licensed 3 February 1626; 1647)

With Francis Beaumont & Philip Massinger

Thierry & Theodoret, tragedy (c. 1607; 1621)
The Coxcomb, comedy (c. 1608–10; 1647)
Beggars' Bush, comedy (c. 1612–13; revised 1622; 1647)
Love's Cure, comedy (c. 1612–13; revised 1625; 1647)

With Philip Massinger

Sir John van Olden Barnavelt, tragedy (August 1619; MS)
The Little French Lawyer, comedy (c. 1619–23; 1647)
A Very Woman, tragicomedy (c. 1619–22; licensed 6 June 1634; 1655)
The Custom of the Country, comedy (c. 1619–23; 1647)
The Double Marriage, tragedy (c. 1619–23; 1647)
The False One, history (c. 1619–23; 1647)
The Prophetess, tragicomedy (licensed 14 May 1622; 1647)
The Sea Voyage, comedy (licensed 22 June 1622; 1647)
The Spanish Curate, comedy (licensed 24 October 1622; 1647)
The Lovers' Progress or The Wandering Lovers, tragicomedy (licensed 6 December 1623; rev 1634; 1647)
The Elder Brother, comedy (c. 1625; 1637)

With Philip Massinger & Nathan Field
The Honest Man's Fortune, tragicomedy (1613; 1647)
The Queen of Corinth, tragicomedy (c. 1616–18; 1647)
The Knight of Malta, tragicomedy (c. 1619; 1647)

With William Shakespeare
Henry VIII, history (c. 1613; 1623)
The Two Noble Kinsmen, tragicomedy (c. 1613; 1634)
Cardenio, tragicomedy (c. 1613)

With Thomas Middleton & William Rowley
Wit at Several Weapons, comedy (c. 1610–20; 1647)

With William Rowley
The Maid in the Mill (licensed 29 August 1623; 1647).

With Nathan Field
Four Plays, or Moral Representations, in One, morality (c. 1608–13; 1647)

With Philip Massinger, Ben Jonson and George Chapman
Rollo Duke of Normandy, or The Bloody Brother, tragedy (c. 1617; revised 1627–30; 1639)

With James Shirley
The Night Walker, or The Little Thief, comedy (c. 1611; 1640)
The Coronation c. 1635

Uncertain
The Nice Valour, or The Passionate Madman, comedy (c. 1615–25; 1647)
The Laws of Candy, tragicomedy (c. 1619–23; 1647)
The Fair Maid of the Inn, comedy (licensed 22 January 1626; 1647)
The Faithful Friends, tragicomedy (registered 29 June 1660; MS.)

The Nice Valour is possibly by Fletcher revised by Thomas Middleton;

The Fair Maid of the Inn is perhaps a play by Massinger, John Ford, and John Webster, either with or without Fletcher's involvement.

The Laws of Candy has been variously attributed to Fletcher and to John Ford.

The Night-Walker was a Fletcher original, with additions by Shirley for a 1639 production.

Even now there is not absolute certainty on several of the plays. The first Beaumont & Fletcher folio of 1647 contained 35 plays and the second folio of 1679 added a further 18. In total 53 plays.

The first folio included The Masque of the Inner Temple and Gray's Inn (1613), and the second The Knight of the Burning Pestle (1607), widely considered Beaumont's solo works, although the latter was in early editions attributed to both writers. Fletcher himself said that Beaumont was attributed so-authorship of many works that belonged solely to Fletcher or to other collaborators.

One play in the canon, Sir John Van Olden Barnavelt, existed in manuscript and was not published till 1883.